The Blood of the Poet

The Blood of the Poet

Selected Poems

William Everson

Edited and with an Afterword
by Albert Gelpi

Broken Moon Press ◆ Seattle

The poems in this collection have been previously published in trade and fine-edition versions. Special thanks to Black Sparrow Press and to New Directions for permission to reprint the poems here.

Printed in the United States of America.

10 9 8 7 6 5 4 3 2 1

ISBN 0-913089-42-7
Library of Congress Catalog Card Number 93-71566

Author photo copyright © 1993 by Daniel Stolpe. Used by permission.
Cover image copyright by Michael Frye/Global Pictures. Used by permission.

Project editor: John Ellison
Copy editor/proofreader: Brandy K. Denisco
Text preparation by: Melissa Shaw

Broken Moon Press
Post Office Box 24585
Seattle, Washington 98124-0585 USA

Contents

The Veritable Years

The Integral Years

The Residual Years

October Tragedy

Do not sing those old songs here tonight.
Outside, the buckeye lifts nude limbs against the moon.
Outside, the heavy-winged herons
Are scaling down into the misty reaches of the marsh.
Bitter is the wind,
And a mad dog howls among the withered elderberry on the ridge.
Bitter is the quiet singing of the cricket,
And the silent pools lie black beneath still reeds.
Go away:
Follow the spoor of a wounded buck,
Over the marsh and deep into the desolate hills.
You must never sing those old songs here again.

Winter Ploughing

Before my feet the ploughshare rolls the earth,
Up and over,
Splitting the loam with a soft tearing sound.
Between the horses I can see the red blur of a far peach orchard,
Half obscured in drifting sheets of morning fog.
A score of blackbirds circles around me on shining wings.
They alight beside me, and scramble almost under my feet
In search of upturned grubs.
The fragrance of the earth rises like tule-pond mist,
Shrouding me in impalpable folds of sweet, cool smell,
Lulling my senses to the rhythm of the running plough,
The jingle of the harness,
And the thin cries of the gleaming, bent-winged birds.

Muscat Pruning

All these dormant fields are held beneath the fog.
The scraggy vines, the broken weeds, the cold moist ground
Have known it now for days.
My fingers are half-numbed around the handles of the shears,
But I have other thoughts.
There is a flicker swooping from the grove on scalloped wings,
His harsh cry widening through the fog.
After his call the silence holds the drip-sound of the trees,
Muffling the hushed beat under the mist.
Over the field the noise of other pruners
Moves me to my work.
I have a hundred vines to cut before the dark.

Attila

On a low Lorrainian knoll a leaning peasant sinking a pit
Meets rotted rock and a slab.
The slab cracks and is split, the old grave opened:
His spade strikes iron and keenly rings.
Out of the earth he picks an ancient sword,
Hiltless with rust and the blade a long double curve,
Steel of no Roman nor Teuton king,
But metal struck in the sleeping East and lost in the raids.
He turns it awhile in the thick hands,
His thumb searching the eaten edge, and throws it aside.
The brown strip winks in the light and is sunk,
Winks once in a thousand years, in the sun and the singing air,
And is lost again in the ground.

Attila, you rode your hordes from the Asian slopes and swept to the
        west,
Roaring down Rome and the north-born Goths.
In the screaming dawns you struck the rich earth and left it smoking;
Struck and butchered and lived like the crimson arc of a cutting knife.
Through the reeling years you ran like a wolf,
Side-slashing blindly from border to border the length of that bleeding
        land,
Till your own lust killed you and the dark swarm broke.

In the nights the moon crawls to the west and is hidden;
The dawns bloom in the east;
The fogs gather.

Attila, in your frenzy of life you burned, but for nothing.
You roared for an instant, shook the world's width, broke the fierce
    tribes.
You are outdone: the earth that you raped has been ravaged more
    foully;
The cities you sacked have been burnt and rebuilt a hundred times;
From your day to this the valleys you plundered
Have known killing and looting, the sharp violence,
The running thunder shaking the night,
A gasping moment of peace and then at it again!

Yet you struck deep: in the fields the earth gives up a curious sword;
The bright-haired folk of a German farm
Regard with doubt a baby born with oval eyes;
In a gusty hut an old man hugs the hearth
And tells an ancient story.

We in the Fields

Dawn and a high film; the sun burned it;
But noon had a thick sheet, and the clouds coming,
The low rain-bringers, trooping in from the north,
From the far cold fog-breeding seas, the womb of the storms.
Dusk brought a wind and the sky opened:
All down the west the broken strips lay snared in the light,
Bellied and humped and heaped on the hills.
The set sun threw the blaze up;
The sky lived redly, banner on banner of far-burning flame,
From south to the north the furnace door wide and the smoke rolling.
We in the fields, the watchers from the burnt slope,
Facing the west, facing the bright sky, hopelessly longing to know the
     red beauty—
But the unable eyes, the too-small intelligence,
The insufficient organs of reception
Not a thousandth part enough to take and retain.
We stared, and no speaking, and felt the deep loneness of
     incomprehension.
The flesh must turn cloud, the spirit, air,
Transformation to sky and the burning,
Absolute oneness with the west and the down sun.
But we, being earth-stuck, watched from the fields,
Till the rising rim shut out the light;
Till the sky changed, the long wounds healed;
Till the rain fell.

August

Smoke-color; haze thinly over the hills, low hanging;
But the sky steel, the sky shiny as steel, and the sun shouting.
The vineyard: in August the green-deep and heat-loving vines
Without motion grow heavy with grapes.
And he in the shining, on the turned earth, loose-lying,
The muscles clean and the limbs golden, turns to the sun the lips and
    the eyes;
As the virgin yields, impersonally passionate,
From the bone core and the aching flesh, the offering.

He has found the power and come to the glory.
He has turned clean-hearted to the last God, the symbolic sun.
With earth on his hands, bearing shoulder and arm the light's touch, he
    has come.
And having seen, the mind loosens, the nerve lengthens,
All the haunting abstractions slip free and are gone;
And the peace is enormous.

Bard

Sing it. Utter the phrase, the fine word.
Make the syllables shout on the page,
The letters form till the line glows and is ringing.
Pursue the illusion. It is sweet to the heart
To think of them listening, to think of them
Thumbing the leaves, the eyes avidly drinking.

You have in your nights the dreams of the older years:
Hearth-side bards in the great halls, singing,
Shouting the tale, chanting the lusty word and the rhyme,
While the warriors stared, the women hushed and not breathing.

It is fine for the heart to think of oneself as the Voice,
The Pointer of Ways.
It is warm in the chest to think of them listening.
Sing the phrase and fashion the line;
Hug the sweet dream in the lonely dusks when the far planes whine in
    the sky and the west deadens.
It is good to the heart, it is fine in the chest to think of them listening.

The Rain on That Morning

We on that morning, working, faced south and east where the sun was
    in winter at rising;
And looking up from the earth perceived the sky moving,
The sky that slid from behind without wind, and sank to the sun,
And drew on it darkly: an eye that was closing.
The rain on that morning came like a woman with love,
And touched us gently, and the earth gently, and closed down
    delicately in the morning,
So that all around were the subtle and intricate touchings.
The earth took them, the vines and the winter weeds;
But we fled them, and gaining the roof looked back a time
Where the rain without wind came slowly, and love in her touches.

Orion

Remote and beyond, lonely farms on the shoulders of hills
Sleep in the night. Seaward-running rivers,
Draining the continental flanks,
Pour in the dark, pour down the mountains,
Suck silt from the plains.
On inland ridges timber stirs in the cloud,
And far down the channels of the southern sky
Those arctic-loving tern are crossing the islands.
Mist gathers; the long shores whiten;
The midnight stars on the central sea
Lure the morning stars over Asia.

Light seeps at the window;
A faded chart of the used season hangs on the wall.
There are mats, worn, the thin bed,
The bare stand holding its chipped jug.
Glow from the alley colors the room: a dull stain.
The tension strung in the nerves of the city
Trembles the night.

Under the crust the massive and dormant stone of the earth
Swings at the core; bulk turns;
The weight turning on the tipped axis hangs to that line;
Atom-smashing pressures war at the center
Straining the charged and furious dark.

We, come at the dead of night
To the stale air of a drab room
High on the edge of the empty street,
Feel under the wind of our own compulsion
Those seekers before in the drained ages,
Daring the dark, daring discovery in the shut rooms,
Secretly meeting at river's edge under scant stars.
They sought and were lucky and achieved fulfillment;
They hung at last on the old fury,
And ground with their loins,
And lay sprawling and nude with their hearts bursting,
Their emptied flesh,
The spent mouths gasping against the dark.

They pound in our limbs at the clenched future.
They drive us above them, beating us up from that dead time,
Thrusting us up to this hanging room,
This toppling night, this act of their need
Forming again from the sunken ages.

Orion! Orion! the swords of the sky!
Forever above the eastern peaks they rise and go over,
Burning and breaking in the random years.
Under their light and the lean of a roof
The eyes drown inward, the blind eyes sinking,
The blind mouths, the great blind currents of the blood pulsing and
    rising.
Here in the room the streams of compulsion
Have formed in the rhythm of these gathering loins;
And feeling behind them the tides of all being—

Betelgeuse his bulk, and the yeared light, and the high silence—
They suck into union,
A part in the torrent of those shattering stars,
And time and space a waveless sea, and the dying suns.
Beyond all the sources of that breeding light
They strike and go out,
To the presence inscrutable and remote awake at the last,
Music that sings at a star's death,
Or the nature of night, that has border nor bulk,
And needs nothing.

Sleep, flesh. Dream deeply, you nerves.
The storms of the north are over Alaska.
This seed of the earth,
This seed of the hungering flesh,
Drives in the growth of the dark.

The Hare: An Earlier Episode

The hare running for life in the sparse growth
Broke cover,
His ears low and his legs driving,
But sure blew the shot,
And shattered and mauled he thrashed in the rubble,
His entrails sprawling the red ruck,
And those angered ants at their work.

Then surely that time
Evil hooded my heart;
Surely that time
The source of all hurt and harm and heavy woe
Pinioned me high in the frozen air,
Gazing far down the blue height of my indifference,
My ears stoppered against those piteous cries
That swam up about me,
My stone eyes cold in my iron face,
The central terror and the separate hurt
Far at my feet.

Between that time and this
The subtle and transigent forces of growth
Have altered my mind;
Nor can I now say the way that it was,
But ice thawed,
Height dwindled,

The dwindling height threw me racked on the ground by that bleeding
    hare,
My torn flesh and splintered bone
Tangled with his.

Against the frozen impossible fact of redemption
(No act undone,
The hare mewling and jerking
Down time from now on)
I draw all my strength,
And wear as I can the measure of pity,
The meed of forbearance,
And the temperance fathered of guilt.

Lava Bed

Fisted, bitten by blizzards,
Flattened by wind and chewed by all weather,
The lava bed lay.
Deer fashioned trails there but no man, ever;
And the fugitive cougars whelped in that lair.
Deep in its waste the buzzards went down to some innominate kill.
The sun fell in it,
And took the whole west down as it died.
Dense as the sea,
Entrenched in its years of unyielding rebuff,
It held to its own.
We looked in against anger,
Beholding that which our cunning had never subdued,
Our power indented,
And only our eyes had traversed.

The Residual Years

As long as we looked lay the low country.
As long as we looked
Were the ranchos miled in their open acres,
The populous oaks and the weedy weirs.
There were birds in the rushes.

And deep in the grass stood the silent cattle.
And all about us the leveled light.
Roads bent to the bogs;
Fenced from the fields they wound in the marshes.
We saw slim-legged horses.

We saw time in the air.
We saw indeed to the held heart of an older order,
That neither our past nor that of our fathers
Knew part in the forming:
An expansive mode remarked through the waste of residual years,
Large in its outline,
Turning up from its depth these traces and wisps
That hung yet on through a cultural close
We had thought too faint to recapture.

The Answer

The bruise is not there,
Nor the bullying boy,
Nor the girl who gave him the bitter gift,
Under the haws in the hollow dark and the windless air;
But the rue remains,
The rue remains in the delicate echo of what was done;
And he who labors above the lines
Leans to an ache as old almost
As the howl that shook him in his own birth,
As the heavy blow that beat him to breath
When the womb had widened.

For boyhood bent him:
Awkward at games he limped in the offing.
Youth yoked him:
The tyrannous sex trenchant between his flowering limbs,
Nor strength to subdue it.
Now manhood makes known the weaknesses flawed in the emergent
    soul:
Guilt marring the vision,
The whimpering lusts and the idiot rages.
And the years gnaw at him.
Deep to the dawns does he marshal all skill at the intractable page,
But nothing converges;
Grown pudgy with time he takes blow and rebuff,
Is baffled,

Hugs to the rind of his crumpled pride,
Endures only out of an obscure persistence
Grained in his soul.

But at last comes a time when, triggered by some inconsequent word,
The breath of an odor,
Some casual touch awakening deep in the somnolent flesh
Its ancient response,
The inner locks open;
And clear down its depth
The delicate structure of that rue harvest
Trembles to life.
The thought stirs in its seed;
The images flower;
Sucked from their secret recesses of mind,
The shadowy traces of all intuition float into being;
And the poem emerges,
Freighted with judgment,
Swung out of the possible into the actual,
As one man's insight matches mankind's at the midpoint of language;
And the meeting minds reduplicate in the running vowel
Their common concern.

Then here rides his triumph:
Caught in his doom he had only his anguish,
But the human pattern imposes across his stammering mind
Its correctional hand.
What was vague becomes strict;
What was personal blooms in the amplification of art;
And the race pronounces;
Out of his mouth there issues the judgment of all mankind,
And he touches attainment in that.

Eastward the Armies

Eastward the armies;
The rumorous dawns seep with the messages of invasion;
The hordes that were held so long in their hate
Are loosed in release.
The South shakes,
The armies awaken;
High in the domed and frozen North the armies engage;
They grope through the hills to the hooded passes;
They meet in the blue and bitter dawns,
And break up in the snow.
To the West: war, war,
The lines down,
The borders broken,
The cities each in its isolation,
Awaiting its end.

Now in my ear shakes the surly sound of the wedge-winged planes,
Their anger brooding and breaking across the fields,
Ignorant, snug in their bumbling idiot dream,
Unconscious of tact,
Unconscious of love and its merciful uses,
Unconscious even of time,
Warped in its error,
And sprawled in exhaustion behind them.

Spring, 1942

The Raid

They came out of the sun undetected,
Who had lain in the thin ships
All night long on the cold ocean,
Watched Vega down, the Wain hover,
Drank in the weakening dawn their brew,
And sent the lumbering death-laden birds
Level along the decks.

They came out of the sun with their guns geared,
Saw the soft and easy shape of that island
Laid on the sea,
An unwakening woman,
Its deep hollows and its flowing folds
Veiled in the garlands of its morning mists.
Each of them held in his aching eyes the erotic image,
And then tipped down,
In the target's trance,
In the ageless instant of the long descent,
And saw sweet chaos blossom below,
And felt in that flower the years release.

The perfect achievement.
They went back toward the sun crazy with joy,
Like wild birds weaving,
Drunkenly stunting;

Passed out over edge of that injured island,
Sought the rendezvous on the open sea
Where the ships would be waiting.

None were there.
Neither smoke nor smudge;
Neither spar nor splice nor rolling raft.
Only the wide waiting waste,
That each of them saw with intenser sight
Than he ever had spared it,
Who circled that spot,
The spent gauge caught in its final flutter,
And straggled down on their wavering wings
From the vast sky,
From the endless spaces,
Down at last for the low hover,
And the short quick quench of the sea.

Chronicle of Division

PART FIVE

Sea:
And in its flaw the sprung silence,
Weighted with dusk,
Margent,
Tufted with shadow,
The skypuffs born of sundown.

Resides:
A vast withholding,
A reticence,
Consuming;
And beckons,
Fleering its white drift,
Its lavish formulation.
Beyond those long stooping ledges,
Those breakers born of the wind's mouth,
The half-light cast like a slick skin
Wrinkles in motion.
And then,
Slowly,
The plumed piling,
The drop,
And the deep west wide-broken,
Split up and spilt,
And the shy casual serene disclosure:
A film at the feet.

What had it done in all its ages?
The same.
Only the same,
Through its grave figuration,
Only the same.
And he nuzzles against its fresh draught,
Turning back and back,
His squinted eyes picking toward west,
Probing its weftage for what it could mean,
For what was in it,
What it held for him,
A possible surcease
From the shadowed doubt
And the shrewd question,
Inhabitant of his heart.

But the letter is there,
Under his hand in the shabby coat,
Like an overlooked clue
In a case disposed long since and forgotten,
Turned up in court.
He fingers its fold,
As if the tips could read for themselves
The dumb script,
Bent in the sheath that bears his name,
That sought him out,
And now mutely waits,
As a restless messenger lolls at the door
Invoking reply.
He makes only the head's gesture,
Shaking off doubt;

The face tilts to the wind,
The searching sight
Preys on contingence,
Its transitory role.

The film.
The long stooping ledges.
The drop.
His eye roves against sundown,
Sets the frail moon in its sky,
That makes its mark,
Emblematic,
In the hesitance of the dusk,
In the approachment of the night,
That swart footfall.
What is he?
Which man of his modes,
Of all he may be,
Shall have knowledge enough,
With the thin sheath in his fingers,
To make any reply?
Not to her, but himself?
Now that the old volcanic hurt,
In its black upheaval,
Buried the civilization of the past?
Now that the Peace,
Breached in the air over Nagasaki,
Lays its ash on the world?
The myriad fragments that make up a war
Come asking home,
Like the unanswerable letter,

In from the islands,
Back from the reefs,
With the foreign sun on their faces,
With the foreign blood on their hands;
Back from the blind insouciant sea,
That sulks and champs and is unconcerned,
Self-caresser,
Forever involved in its own immolation:
Seminal jell on the dappled shore
Sufficing: its adequate own.

The film.
The long stooping ledges.
The drop.
And the vague sand run through the fingers.
But the solitary self under the wind's eye.
The self and the self,
The divisible selves,
Ill-eased with each other.
There mumbles the sea.
(Dip down, dip down)
There mumbles the sea,
But a mnemic speech that never comes clear.
And the solitary self
Broods on its track,
The footprint on the glistening berm,
Easily erased.
A sandpiper,
In his hunched run,
Looks over his shoulder.

(Dip down, dip down)
The lurch rhythm and the dull beat
Tramp out the pace of the blood's scansion.
The dead warriors of all the past,
In a ragged surge at the raw future,
Plunge and fall back.

His slow hand picks up a stone,
Thumbs the scuffed edge;
Wave-work,
That has taken away,
Left its crease and its wrinkle,
And restored nothing.
But brings out a beauty.
See, yes, the fine seam.
A flaw, yes, but of beauty.
His.
If he wants.
If he wills.

He raises his head.
The wondering face
Turns and deflects.
And the sudden hand
Hangs like a hawk
To broach an exacerbate need.

The film.
The long stooping ledges.
The drop.
And the hand falls,

Rips open and enters,
Invading the storehouse of the breast,
Where the old acquisitions
Lie heaped in its hold.

Dip down! Dip down!

Raids and ransacks,
Rakes up its rich hoard,
The greenful seasons,
Vineyard and valley,
The good and the glad.

Dip down! Dip down!

The face in its speechless joy,
Caught up and made whole,
Seen,
Flung in the wind's fluff,
Brought back.

Dip down! Dip down!

And the clear song,
And the plenitude of touch,
And the face.

Dip down!

And the rapturous body,
Its naked divestment,
Its total request.

Who claims this guilty?
Who brands this bad?

Dip down!

The plundering hand,
Like a mad king,
Reels through the rooms,
Seizes and shakes and finds no clue,
Loots to the last,
Descends to the sunken tomb in the self,
The trapdoor clamped in the murky cellar,
Heaves open its hole,
Drops keening down;
And there discerns,
On the tumorous wall,
Like a human skin
Peeled from the flesh and stretched up to dry,
The raw map of the world.
The shorelines, etched like flaring nerves,
Chart their red coasts.
In the meridians of death
The veined rivers bleed to the sea.
Blotched through the hemispheric zones
The purplish bruise of a total war
Festers and seethes.

How comes it here?
Who made it, the map,
Skinned from the torn flesh of the world,
Hung up in the heart
To blanch the face and blind the eye?
Is this his own handwork,
Who grubbed out the years in the squalid camps
With the men who denied—
Cried: No! Cried: Not to make murder!
Sucked in asleep with a fat wage and a mother's kiss!—
Who lived to verify the slave
And lip the pauper's oath?

Oh, ask up an answer!
Ask each and any!
Strike innocence out of the human page!
Ask the illiterate dead,
Parched and rotten in the clogged earth,
Mummied stiff in the black tombs,
Ploughed in the sand,
Chewed and tattered in the gnawing wave,
Dissolved in the high exploding air
To sift on the cities themselves had burned!
Ask each and any!
Jehovah, who lulls them all in his hallowed palm!
Dealer in mercy and dealer in wrath!
Sweet Jesus, boned and gutted on the phallic tree!
Open your blood-filled mouth and speak!

The sandpiper's cry,
Flung over his back,
Stringes the sea-voice.
The round eye
Gams and glitters,
And stares him down.
In the necropolic heart,
Where crime and repentance
Merge in the attitudes of fear;
Where pity and hate
Grope together and are one;
Where wisdom,
Sprawled like a bayoneted priest,
Raises its face
To speak once more and once more be struck—
The great hide of the map
Oozes and drains,
And all the forsaken immitigable dead
Groan in their fitful sleep.

Why? How and by whom?
What blind intercession
Culls precedence out,
Stalks through the cleftage of event,
Tracks finally to earth?
What merciless equation
Couples A with X
To prove B guilty?
What savage disseverance
Rives agent from act,
Leaves the pregnable seed

Its huge germination,
Its terrible fruit?

Oh, deep down and dredged!
The sanguinary laughter,
The immoderate mirth!
The thick guggle of all taken attempt,
Deflected endeavor,
Swept out and dispersed,
Ground in the black bowels of decision
And heaped on the strand!

He chokes.
Cramped in convulsion he coughs, he gags,
Hacking the phlegm up from the heart,
From the heavy lung,
That breeds its deep bile,
And is spat;
And steps over that stain,
And leaves it there on the glistening shale
Where the sea bird shat,
Where the sand crab's sucked pathetic shell,
Ironic chrysalis,
Heels in the blistering wind.

The great trampling rote.
The outward-running suck.
The huge silence hung over sound.
The excoriate eye.

The self's knowledge in the self's lack,
And the riddle of error.

The hand checks and falters,
And is withdrawn,
Shriveled.
Deep in the west the open range and pasture of the wind
Ripples and flows;
Those palisaded cliffs that flank the south
Will be ankled in dusk but their crowns gilded;
Far out now and under
The pouring light drops ever away,
The black racer sweeping along the sea,
A sliding wedge,
And the wedge widens,
The blade,
Made steep,
Thickened,
The coast covered,
All taken,
Blacked out and bound,
Wholly annulled
In the swift totalitarian seizure of the night.

Not yet, not yet.
Nor all the impulsion of the mind,
That beggars completion,
Fans it the faster.

And daylight or dark,
It's all one to the sea,
That has beach to dapple.
And yet, when the wind's right,
And the voice muffled,
Maybe deep toward dawn
When the sad moon lays on the sea its glimmering track
And the great bulk shuffles,
Then, then does the self,
That so needs knowledge,
That so wants to know,
Draw as on some shimmering dream
That long ago had steeped the mind in its potent drench
And been forgotten;
And glimmers again in the moon's track;
And is maybe the meaning of the self,
It, too, oceanic,
A central rest and a surface trouble,
And always at flux,
From pleasure to pain,
And out of the pain to painful pleasure,
And so back to pain.

But never for sure.
Not on the shoreline,
Where the shells,
Loose change in the wave's purse,
A counterfeit coin,
Rustle and toss;
Not far at sea where the cormorant steers his undeviate course
To the specific rock;

Nor among those banded gulls,
Keeping their careful withdrawal,
Their fleeting shadows ghosts of the wave,
Holding that shifting dangerous edge
Severe in the tilted bill and the tucked feet—
This too,
These too,
Would write,
Like the wind,
Upon his heart
Their uneasy answer,
And watch him over his mute years,
With the round regarding eye,
And keep their distance.

Such would he know,
And hold the disconsolate disclosure under his hand,
To wear the incertitude,
Thin glove against guilt
That sleeps,
Like the winter bear,
In the cavern cut in the heart
By the impassive year.

But now the thunder is all converged for sundown,
And the wind smokes on those ledges,
In that wild beckon,
The whitecap's unquestionable wish,
Where all consequence lurks,
Inchoate,
Like a possible synthesis of the self,

And is so revealed,
The metaphor in the sea's mouth,
And is his reprieve.

The film.
The long stooping ledges.
The drop.
He lifts up his hand,
Its shadow flitting between the indefinite face and the down sun;
And he turns,
And goes then,
With the salt smell in his coat,
With the crumpled letter,
With the restless pebble at odd's end in the bare pocket;
And will watch once more from the flinted path in the cliff-cut,
Where it lies out there now far away as in sleep and untroubled;
And weeks later,
Risen at dawn,
Will trace in the rife electric air
That imperative presence,
And suddenly all the tensile might
Will shift and settle;
He will kneel to its print,
Its fluent gesture: the fine sand
Strewn on the rug from the fluted cuff,
From the frayed cloth.

Cascade Locks, Oregon

In the Fictive Wish

So him in dream
Does celibate wander,
Where woman waits,
Of whom he may come to,
Does woman wait,
Who now is
Of his.

Does woman wait.
Not wife now;
Long gone,
Face fading;
Of her once surely,
Whom best he knew,
But not now.
Nor any girl in his life known.
Of them too as of wife maybe,
But not wholly;
And now not.

In him lives alone and is his;
Was always,
Who looked for her outward.
Mistook her,
Wife's face and friend's;

This one's pace and that one's saunter;
Finds now,
In long abstention,
Own form and feature,
Not others,
Laughing behind his thought;
But solemn mostly,
Waiting within.

Once on a paper he drew her face;
First knew then her nature;
His in himself.

Water-woman,
Near water or of it,
The sea-drenched hair;
Of gray gaze and level
Mostly he knows her;
Of such bosom as face would fade in;
Of such thigh as would fold;
Of huge need come to;
Man out of heart's hurt come,
Of self divided.
Her certain shape:
Of such body, yes, and of such croft,
Where ache of sex could so conjoin,
Could so sink,
As soul sinks enfolded,
In dream sunken;
Of such cunted closure,
Butt broad in the love-grip;

As of bed,
Broad,
As of width for woman;
And of belly
Broad for the grapple.

But of grave smiling eyes,
Of gaze gray,
Veiled;
Of such soul;
Oh, surely of such other self,
As he in life sought so to have
And could not;
So looked from such eyes,
Of such gaze made;
And of mouth
Lipped for laughter;
And deep-breasted,
As all women would be:
Of such, she.

But never of need,
Nor begs;
Waits only,
As does water,
And may be entered.

Wader,
Watcher by wave,
Woman of water;

Of speech unknown,
Of nothing spoken.

But waits.

And he has,
And has him,
And are completed.

So she.

II

But masked of the self,
And in it,
What is she?
Who?
Of wife's face divested,
Of friend's feature,
What must she presage?
Fair-countenanced she,
And the bodily grace;
Sleep-comer;
Lurker behind the veils of thought,
And is laughing;
Or grave-smiler there in his deep trances.
Not composite?
For seems she rather
As if was always,
And herself seized on image
When it came near

For use of it,
To make it her own.
Was not all he did
With that other, his wife,
Whom in time he loved wholly,
His huge effort to make them one?
All his watching,
Over their fruit in the sun-filled mornings,
Or in lamp's light of evening
When night laid its indivisible mark on the world,
Was it not surely his need
To find the woman within
In the woman without?
All his rapture in love,
Was it not precisely
When such an accord
Was most complete?
Then most was her breast
Ease of his need,
And the thigh a solace,
And the sudden laugh he loved,
When what looked from her eyes,
As of some clarity of self
Unbeknownst even to her,
But was there,
And he saw it,
And it was—
All transformed!
Then was she not
Most wholly embodied
In what was his?

Till celibacy's long withdrawal
Let down the mask;
And he came in his dream,
Or even in waking,
There in the gloom by the swart tree,
Face to face with one
Stranger than any,
And dearer,
And indeed the pure substance
Of all he sought.

III

But now having seen,
And known at last of his own and none other,
Does she not frighten?
When he leans to embrace,
To merge him into her,
Nurtured of need,
Her deep-biding grace and her bodily essence,
Of grave-smiling aspect and of comforting gaze,
Then does she not terrify?

For whom now may he love?
Whoever incites,
Knows only of her,
And hence of him,
And not another;
Of such multiple visage,
Yet not another.

Blue eye or gray and the body's breathing—
What wonder of woman,
Now that he knows,
In whom touch dwells,
And all emptiness fills,
Can he come to;
Of such utter unlikeness,
In that hope of the heart,
Achieved at last in its own desolation,
Such wild reparation!
Nursed in the mind,
And so disheveled!
None! Oh, none!
She lives in them all,
In his eyes looking out,
Herself emplanting!
Her glance is there!
Her firmness of tread and her sure survival!
She lives!
And the master motive,
Her womanhood's weal,
To so dissemble,
To so disenchant of his huge rapture,
Being of dream only,
And not of his having,
Save there,
Where no substance is,
Nor touch obtains;
But the skinnied heart
Wisps out its want in the fictive wish,

And is revealed;
And in that revelation
Betrays.

    IV

Wader,
Watcher by water,
Walker alone by the wave-worn shore,
In water woven.

She moves now where the wave glistens,
Her mouth mocking with laughter,
In the slosh unheard
When the sea slurs after;
In the sleepy suckle
That laps at her heel where the ripple hastens.

And the laughing look laid over her arm,
A tease and a wooing,
Through that flying maze when the wave falls forward,
From its faultless arch, from its tallest yearn
To its total ruin.

Lurker,
She leaves with laughter,
She fades where the combers falter,
Is gone as the wave withdrawing
Or the sleeper's murmur;
Is gone as the wave withdrawing
Sobs on the shore, and the stones are shaken;

As the ruined wave
Sucks and sobs in the rustling stones,
When the tide is taken.

Cascade Locks, Oregon

The Blowing of the Seed

IV

If you were to try to say,
Half-closing your eyes in the way you have,
Your mouth pulled in a bit in its pre-speech purpose . . .

If you were to turn your face to me,
That sudden look of inward revelation,
When out of so much of thought, so much of thinking—
Out of your nights, as you lie abed and pick up the pieces;
Out of your days;
Over whatever task it is you are doing, in whatever place,
Going about your unguessable business
With that air of half-abstraction,
Half-involvement . . .

If you were to lift up your face,
And from so dense a demand, so deep a denial;
From your hemmed and hampered past,
When your world was weak,
And all your instance
Turned on the tremble of a touch,
And you had no grip, no grasp . . .

If you were to break,
The tears beat from your eyes;
All your hard hurt broke open and bared
In its sudden gust of bleak exposure . . .

If you were to try . . .

Under my hand your heart hits like a bird's,
Hushed in the palms, a muffled flutter,
And all the instinct of its flight
Shut in its wings.

      v

And then that humming,
In the tenseness under the skin,
Where the little nerves
Mesh, merge:
In that fabric, that suture,
Where time runs out his rapid dance
And pain poises—

There. There.

Under those roots the running of it
Wakens a wind to skirl in the grasses,
A rain dance of wind;
A long passion forming out of its farther region;
A past of such pain,
Of such deprivation;
Out of such hunted hope when none could be had,
But yet the hope, the hunger;
Out of such starting
That wind widens,
That wind weaves.

Cry out, cry out,
Speak from the bloodied past, the failured venture;
Speak from the broken vows and the shattered pledges;
Speak from the ruined marriage of flesh
Where joy danced and was denied,
And the harsh croppage of time
Reaped its rue in those dolorous arches.

Dance. Dance.
Dance out the troubled dream.
Dance out the murderous pain,
The mutilated silence.
Dance out the heart in its narrow hole
Caught in the clamp of that brittle hunger.
Dance in the rags of an old remorse,
In the tattered garments of trust,
Ripped from the narrow thighs,
Thrown to the crickets.
Dance and be spent;
Fall in the long gasp,
The heart too hurt, the spirit
Cut too quick—

All gone, all broken,
Smashed and smithereened.
And none to know, ever;
None to heed.

Be through with it then.
Be finished.
Close out and complete.

Look. I am come.
Like a whirlwind
Mounting out of a foaming sea.
I suck all inward.
I shriek.

Dance! Dance!
Dance out the sad bereavement of flesh,
The broken suture.
Dance out the weight of the prone years.
Dance out denial.
Dance it out in the heave of that hope,
Sprung from the proud immortal flesh
That shoots up its flower.
Dance out the sharp damnation of time
That sets the crow's-foot
Crafty under the blear eye
And has its instance.
Dance it out, all,
And be brought low,
And be low broken,
And be brinked.

Now in a black time I come to you
Crouched in your corner of hut by your meager blaze.
Now like a man out of a madded dream
I come from my cleavage.
I come running across the flints and notches of a glacial year.
I bear brash on my back.
I wear an old woe.

Be joined.
Be clipped.
Be crouched and crotched,
Woman, woman!

Bring me that moaning mouth: I stop it.
Bring me the knock of that hurt-impacted heart:
I grind it out.

I level.
I level the last of my life in your life.
I hammer harsher than hooves.
I gnaw like knives.

Give me that past and that pain-proud flesh.
I come with the hurled and howling north:
A mad naked man.

VI

Of such touch given;
Of such sight—
Your eyes, where the warmth lives on from a late loving,
And your palms,
Placed—

Speak you?

That word wears out the woe of the world.

But now as your mouth on it shapes for a sound,
As a sign,
As of some sign given
Long ago, between man, between woman,
So on your lip it loudens,
Through those chambers of the mind
Where all past in its slumber
Lives on, lives on.

You speak.

And the chimes,
The bronze bells of those death-departed years
Are all awakened.

The Dusk

The light goes: that once powerful sun,
That held all steeples in its grasp,
Smokes on the western sea.
Under the fruit tree summer's vanishing residuum,
The long accumulation of leaf,
Rots in the odor of orchards.
Suddenly the dark descends,
As on the tule ponds at home the wintering blackbirds,
Flock upon flock, the thousand-membered,
In for the night from the outlying ploughlands,
Sweep over the willows,
Whirled like a net on the shadowy reeds,
All wings open.
It is late. And any boy who lingers on to watch them come in
Will go hungry to bed.
But the leaf-sunken years,
And the casual dusk, over the roofs in a clear October,
Will verify the nameless impulse that kept him out
When the roosting birds and the ringing dark
Dropped down together.

The Veritable Years

Triptych for the Living

III. THE WISE

> *Behold, there came wise men from the East*
> *to Jerusalem, saying Where is He. . . ?*

Miles across the turbulent kingdoms
They came for it, but that was nothing;
That was the least. Drunk with vision,
Rain stringing the ragged beards,
When a beast lamed they caught up another
And goaded west.

For the time was on them.
Once, as it may, in the life of a man;
Once, as it was, in the life of mankind,
All is corrected. And their years of pursuit,
Raw-eyed reading the wrong texts,
Charting the doubtful calculations—
Those nights knotted with thought,
When dawn held off, and the rooster
Rattled the leaves with his blind assertion—
All that, they regarded, under the Sign,
No longer as search but as preparation.
For when the mark was made *they* saw it.
Nor stopped to reckon the fallible years,
But rejoiced and followed,
And are called wise, who learned that Truth,
When sought and at last seen,
Is never found. It is given.

And they brought their camels
Breakneck into that village,
And flung themselves down in the dung and dirt of that place,
And kissed that ground, and the tears
Ran on the face where the rain had.

from

The Falling of the Grain

V. IN THE RIPENESS OF THE WEED

And now it is summer.
And the strong weed
Shoulders the fence,
And the weak weed
Scatters,
And all things
Hold increase.
And the summer
Burns, and I remember mornings
Risen one from another,
But must put aside that thought now,
Save maybe in rising
To note but the single
Print in the bed.

But there is a greater
Glory that one may come to,
Whence even that other
Gets its flame.

This we take.

Therefore do I salute that magic of yours
This last time in my poems, my wife—
We who clasped in the high try at holiness
Where holiness never could be;

And are now, since we must, at last content,
To seek where it more purely is.

And the strong weed
Seeds, and the weak weed
Scatters, and I see in them each
A glory of God;
And am made grateful,
That of His help
Can put down now the pride of the flesh
(Which had not, heretofore, been my ability)
And am humbled,
And not given to rankling
(As I was)
When the ripe weed
Seeds, and the weak weed
Scatters.

VI. THE BURNING BOOK

Now it may happen that one
Who is himself a binder of books,
Sometimes, too rough with the needle,
May pierce to his hand, and by chance from that pierce
Let fall his blood in the book;
Then does he, seeing it,
Cast out that leaf as blemished,
Because there is blood on it.

But in the book I bind for you
Rather do I now take up that leaf
And bind it in. For as our blood
On the leaf of this life is surely no blemish to God,
So do I trust that my blood in this book
Will be no blemish to you.

For it is by blood that we are made dear.

It is by the blood of Our Lord each day in the Mass
That we are perfectly endeared to God;
And therefore will it be by the mingling
Of His blood with ours on the smutched page
Of our life, that we may hope to see endeared
The smutched page of mankind in that otherwise
Blemishless book of His Works.

And as my blood is alone on the leaf,
So on the leaf of this life
Must it also remain alone from yours.
Yet do I pray that in the broader Book
May these mingle, and be altogether
Quenched in that brighter Blood,
Which burns, and is the true
Letter of life,
And pure on the page
Makes up the rare
Rubrication of the Word.

The Screed of the Flesh

Be not as the horse and mule,
that have no understanding.
— PSALM XXXI

I cried out to the Lord
That the Lord might open the wall of my heart
And show me the thing I am.

All of my life I walked in the world
But I had not understanding.

All of my life I gloried self,
Singing the glory of myself;
I let the exuberance of the self, the passion of self,
Serve for my full sufficiency.

But all of my life I knew not what I was:
The thing I was, it had not understanding.
It ran like the colt in the field,
That takes its delight in the pluck-up of its foot,
In the looseness of its mane;
That takes its pleasure in the lift of knee,
The liquid action of the knee;

And has no end except its running as its end,
Nor asks of what it runs, nor where;
But runs, and takes its glory
In the swiftness of its run.

So I. I took my glory
In the running of the heart,
Knowing it good;
And darkled my days with ignorance.

I darkled the fields of my childhood,
The country roads of my young manhood,
And the streets, the streets of my full maturity.
All these, the darkling days of my ignorance.
And did run, and reveled in the run.
And knew not where I ran, nor why,
Nor toward what thing I ran.

I ran, but I had not understanding.

As the greyhound runs, as the jackrabbit runs in the jimson;
As the kestrel flies, as the swamphawk flies on the tules;
As the falcon stoops in the dawn, as the owl strikes in the dusk;
I flew, but I never knew the face of the Light that I flew in.

Lord, Lord, as the coupling horse, as the bull and the ram,
Who cover, and who dispel themselves in the creature of their kind,
And fall back, and the seed of their kind is left in the creature of their
     kind,

But they know it not: the waste of the seed of the self
Stains in the shaggy hide, and they know it not.
I stood in the stain of my own seed and had not understanding.
I lay in the coals of my burning, and knew but that I was burnt.
I had not understanding.

And when I stooped to drink at the cistern could not but quench my
     thirst.
Nor when I ate of the pomegranate, nor when I tasted of the grape,
(The muscat or the sultana, the malaga or the black);
When I crushed in my mouth the fat of their mast,
Could not, could not but eat. Ate only. I had not understanding.
Nor gave I thanks, nor the thought of thanks,
Nor spoke up, ever, my debt of thanks, as each day
I was endebted, as each day I could only be
By the free spilth of Thy giving.

Lord, Lord, I ate, but I had not understanding.

          ◆

For how shall the eater who eats but the passable thing of the earth
Be filled with his act of eating?
Belly will fill; blood will fill of the eaten thing; body will fill.
Bowels will fill of the eaten thing; dung be given back to the earth
That the eatable thing might be.
Earth consumes and sea consumes and the element of air consumes;
So shall the perishing things of the self return to the things they are.

For what did I hope of this thing of self that I sought to give it glory?
Did I think this lovely thing the flesh is more than of dung that is
     dropped?

Did I think the flight of the hastening foot, the lilt in it, the leap that
   is there;
Did I think the beautiful breathing of runners is more than the stain
   of their sweat?

For the earth assumes these things of its own, taking them back.
It takes up the things of which it is made, it forever recovers.
Sea recovers, air recovers the spending breath of runners.
Each recovers its own; each receives it back.
The beauty of running men and of beasts, the gleam of the horse and
   the whippet;
The music of woman in motion, that wink of the heel and the arm,
The waist that is supple and drawn—O glory of earth
In the pulse of the carrying knee! O, glory of God-created earth
In the pace of the fabled ankles!

These are the things we have as the earth, as the shimmer of earth has
   our love.
And these the earth recovers, for these are the things of its own.
All these does the earth recover, the earth and the air and the sea; each
   assumes them back;
Almost as if they were never meant to be more than the thing they were
   made of,
Nothing more than earth, than air, nor anything more than sea.
As if the earth begrudged them, and badly wanted them back.
As the earth wants back the ash of the grass in the smoking fields of
   October,
When the sun-struck face of the hill is burnt to make for the pastures of
   spring;
As the earth wants back the black on the rocks when the hill is burnt
   for pasture.

There the bull's head falls on the stubble, the bone of the bull is tossed;
The sheep's head gleams on the hill where the skulking cougar
    dropped it;
The bones lie white and scattered, the slotted hooves lie thrown.

(And the dawn coyotes
Snuff them, and pass
Over them, and are gone.
They go like smoke in the thickets.
The hunger of beasts
Snuffs dried bone on the hill;
For the hunger of beasts
Is filled with the flesh of beasts,
But the flesh of the beast will fade.
The hunger of beasts will find no filling
When the flesh of the beast is gone.)

I lay on the hill as a beast of the hill which I knew as the hill beast
    knows.
I sang as the linnet, that sings from a throbbing pride of self
Just to be singing. I sang as a bird, that bursts with a bigness of heart,
And makes it to sing, nor ever asks of the source of its song,
But sings for the singing. I sang on the steepness of the hill
Nor knew why I sang.

Lord, Lord, I sang, but I had not understanding.
Lord, Lord, I sang, but the mouth of my soul was shut.

      ◆

The mouth of my soul was utterly stopped with the wadded rag of my
    self,
As the truthful man who would speak of truth is gagged and kept from
    speaking;
As the mouth of a man of terrible truths is stuffed with a wad of rags,
So I gagged my soul with the stuff of self, I gagged it and led it away.
I took it down to the cellars of self where the ear of the mind is deaf;
To the clay and earthy walls of my pride where the sewer sucked in the
    dark;
Where the gross spore lurked on the table and the lewd spore throve
    underfoot;
Where the rat-wad dried on the dish and the mouse-print slept in the
    dust;
Where the things of the self were wholly contained in the world of its
    own creation,
There did I gag the truthful voice that it might not ever be heard.

I had a savior in my soul
But I riddled his brow with prickles.
I had a good redeemer
But I nailed him to a post.

And I threw his body down in the dark that the drains might drain it
    away,
That the restless sea might eat of it and the eating earth erase,
That the death air of the cellar might wholly dispel its voice.
For the earth and the air and the salt of the sea will take of their own
    and dispel it,
The things that are truly of their own, each will surely dispel.
And I gave that good redeemer up for the act of their dispelling.

But earth and air would not dispel, nor the sharp-set salt of the sea.
None of these would dispel him, on him they would not work.
For the leaching acids within the earth, they would not eat of my soul,
Nor would the salt sea stanch it, nor would the air erode.
The very iron of earth they eat, the hard gem and the agate;
But the soul that I sank in the drains of self, of this they would not eat.

But it rose from the swirling dust, it rose from the salt of the sea;
It walked on the swirling water, it stood on the sound of the sea.
And the air made room to pass it, the raw air turned aside;
The wind it would not take it, the air it let it be.

                                        It said:
O one not made of matter, on you I hold no claim!

And the earth cried out, and the sea cried, and the salts of the earth,
    they cried;
The acids that are of earth, they cried; they cried, and they would not
    eat.
I sank my soul in the salt of the sea, and the very sea disclaimed it.

And gave it back,
Casting it.
As at the recession of waters
The live thing
Lay on the edge of the sea.
And the sea lapped it,
And it lifted,
It put up its head—

As the worm,
Knocked out of the apple,
Lifts up its head,
So did it lift.

So did it lift up its own limp head
And open its own blear eye.
The soul that was given back from the sea
Looked up, to know itself not of the dead.
The soul looked up from the slime of the self
And opened its own blear eye,
Crying:
Spare Thou, O God, the thing that I am,
And give me to know my condition!

Lord, Lord, I cried in my heart
For I had not understanding.

◆

For I never had been of His knowledge, nor was I yet of His way,
Nor knew His way was the way of man, and His way the way of the
    soul.
For I saw not other than the horse or the mule, and these have not
    understanding.
I suffered but as the suffering mule, and sweat as the field horse sweats,
Who all day long must plod in the field, and know not why he drives,
But surely the bit will break his jaw, save but that he drives.
And the sweat of the horse makes a salt on him that dries in the
    bleaching sun,
So my sweat made stiff the garment of soul with the stiffening salt
    of the self.

And I labored, and I did lift, I trudged as the field horse trudges.
I sweated beside the sweating horse and the two sweats fell together.
And I saw there was no distinction, we were made as one in our sweat.
And I loved the horse as I loved myself, for our sweat had proved us
    one.

And I rose up from my coupling, with my seed that dried on my flesh;
And I saw the horse in his couple, and his seed, it also dried.
We poured out our sweat and our seed, and this had proved us one.
I held myself but as the horse, and was content in his lot,
To sweat in the leather and bite the bit, and turn to salt of the earth;
As the salt of my sweat fell down on the earth, with the salt of the earth
    made one;
As the salt of the horse fell down and was one with the single salt of the
    earth;
When the horse, his knees failed of driving, lay down and died on the
    earth;
That the earth and the air might have him, that the sea might assume
    him back;
So did I stop the mouth of my soul and lay it down by the horse.
For I loved the horse as I loved the earth, and the soul I would give
    back.

But the earth would not assume it, the sea would not, nor the air.

Lord, Lord, I lay my soul on the empty earth,
For I had not understanding.

    ◆

And what was the meaning of my soul
That was no thing of the earth?
That was no thing of the volatile air
And nothing of the sea?
For nowhere that I probed and looked
Could I find for its last place.
It was not made for this earthly earth,
It was not made for this sea.

And I cried to the Lord
That He show me the thing
That truly He meant me to be:

Made me a thing to live on earth,
But somehow not be of it.

Made me of earth and eating earth,
And somehow not be of it.

To in time lie down as the horse lies down,
But never to be of it.

Given back as the mule is given,
But never end within it.

I cried to the Lord
That the Lord might show me the thing I am—

He showed me my soul!

A Canticle to the Waterbirds

Clack your beaks you cormorants and kittiwakes,
North on those rock-croppings finger-jutted into the rough Pacific
    surge;
You migratory terns and pipers who leave but the temporal clawtrack
    written on sandbars there of your presence;
Grebes and pelicans; you comber-picking scoters and you shorelong
    gulls;
All you keepers of the coastline north of here to the Mendocino
    beaches;
All you beyond upon the cliff-face thwarting the surf at Hecate Head;
Hovering the under-surge where the cold Columbia grapples at the
    bar;
North yet to the Sound, whose islands float like a sown flurry of chips
    upon the sea;
Break wide your harsh and salt-encrusted beaks unmade for song
And say a praise up to the Lord.

And you freshwater egrets east in the flooded marshlands skirting the
    sea-level rivers, white one-legged watchers of shallows;
Broad-headed kingfishers minnow-hunting from willow stems on
    meandering valley sloughs;
You too, you herons, blue and supple-throated, stately, taking the air
    majestical in the sunflooded San Joaquin,
Grading down on your belted wings from the upper lights of sunset,
Mating over the willow clumps or where the flatwater rice fields
    shimmer;
You killdeer, high night-criers, far in the moon-suffusion sky;

Bitterns, sand-waders, all shore-walkers, all roost-keepers,
Populates of the 'dobe cliffs of the Sacramento:
Open your water-dartling beaks,
And make a praise up to the Lord.

For you hold the heart of His mighty fastnesses,
And shape the life of His indeterminate realms.
You are everywhere on the lonesome shores of His wide creation.
You keep seclusion where no man may go, giving Him praise;
Nor may a woman come to lift like your cleaving flight her clear
    contralto song
To honor the spindrift gifts of His soft abundance.
You sanctify His hermitage rocks where no holy priest may kneel to
    adore, nor holy nun assist;
And where His true communion-keepers are not enabled to enter.

And well may you say His praises, birds, for your ways
Are verved with the secret skills of His inclinations,
And your habits plaited and rare with the subdued elaboration of His
    intricate craft;
Your days intent with the direct astuteness needful for His outworking,
And your nights alive with the dense repose of His infinite sleep.
You are His secretive charges and you serve His secretive ends,
In His clouded, mist-conditioned stations, in His murk,
Obscure in your matted nestings, immured in His limitless ranges.
He makes you penetrate through dark interstitial joinings of His
    thicketed kingdoms,
And keep your concourse in the deeps of His shadowed world.

Your ways are wild but earnest, your manners grave,
Your customs carefully schooled to the note of His serious mien.
You hold the prime condition of His clean creating,
And the swift compliance with which you serve His minor means
Speaks of the constancy with which you hold Him.
For what is your high flight forever going home to your first
    beginnings,
But such a testament to your devotion?
You hold His outstretched world beneath your wings, and mount upon
    His storms,
And keep your sheer wind-lidded sight upon the vast perspectives of
    His mazy latitudes.

But mostly it is your way you bear existence wholly within the context
    of His utter will and are untroubled.
Day upon day you do not reckon, nor scrutinize tomorrow, nor
    multiply the nightfalls with a rash concern,
But rather assume each instant as warrant sufficient of His final seal.
Wholly in Providence you spring, and when you die you look on death
    in clarity unflinched,
Go down, a clutch of feather ragged upon the brush;
Or drop on water where you briefly lived, found food,
And now yourselves made food for His deep current-keeping fish, and
    then are gone:
Is left but the pinion-feather spinning a bit on the uproil
Where lately the dorsal cut clear air.

You leave a silence. And this for you suffices, who are not of the
    ceremonials of man,
And hence are not made sad to now forgo them.
Yours is of another order of being, and wholly it compels.

But may you, birds, utterly seized in God's supremacy,
Austerely living under His austere eye—
Yet may you teach a man a necessary thing to know,
Which has to do of the strict conformity that creaturehood entails,
And constitutes the prime commitment all things share.
For God has given you the imponderable grace to *be* His verification,
Outside the mulled incertitude of our forensic choices;
That you, our lessers in the rich hegemony of Being,
May serve as testament to what a creature is,
And what creation owes.

Curlews, stilts and scissortails, beachcomber gulls,
Wave-haunters, shore-keepers, rockhead-holders, all cape-top
    vigilantes,
Now give God praise.
Send up the strict articulation of your throats,
And say His name.

The Encounter

My Lord came to me in the deep of night;
The sullen dark was wounded with His name.
I was as woman made before His eyes;
My nakedness was as a secret shame.
I was a thing of flesh for His despise;
I was a nakedness before His sight.

My Lord came to me in my depth of dross;
I was as woman made and hung with shame.
His lip sucked up the marrow of my mind,
And all my body burned to bear His name.
Upon my heart He placed His pouring pain;
I hung upon Him as the albatross
Hangs on the undering gale and is sustained.

My Lord came to me and I knew, I knew.
I was a uselessness and yet He came
Shafted of the center of the sun.
I was a nakedness and was of shame;
I was a nothingness and unbegun.
The look He leaned upon me lit me through.

My Lord came to me in my own amaze;
My body burned and that was of my shame.
I who was too impure to meet His gaze
Bent beneath the impress of His name.

He broke beyond the burning and the blame,
And burned the blame to make that pain of praise.

My Lord went from me and I could not be.
I fell through altitudes of leveled light,
As, shaken into space from his mast-tree,
The lookout falls unto the patient sea,
Falling forever through Time's windless flight
To meet the waters of eternity.

The Cross Tore a Hole

A Canticle for the Feast of the Most Precious Blood, 1954.

> *There are three who give testimony in heaven:*
> *the Father, the Word, and the Holy Ghost:*
> *and these three are one.*
>
> *And there are three that give testimony on earth:*
> *the spirit, the water and the blood:*
> *and these three are one.*
>
> —THE FIRST EPISTLE OF ST. JOHN

From his tall masted Tree
The Lover looks on life.
His smile replenishes the gaze of miles,
His look renews the sun.

Tall on his Tree
The Son of Man breathes life.
His gritted gasp,
The long life-going,
Pants its full pang,
Breathes in earth's dead lung,
The seedcake of his kiss
Tongued in the Beloved's lips,
His given gift.

(Deep down earth aches.
Her womb wakes up.
Bright-breast she stirs.
Womb-wise, she waits.)

At three o'clock in the afternoon
The centuries
Groined on the ruinous spar
Lunge toward life.

Tall on its straining stalk
The seed-sack of Christ's body,
Swollen with thick
Regenerative blood,
Swells and distends.
Engulfed in sky it strains.
The hot clouds press it round.
The birth-panged earth
Hurls and uproils,
Cracks her rude mortices.
Here at the straining tip
The Nerve of God
Quicks in its ecstasy.
The forward-crowding centuries,
Eons of man's act,
Lunge and crack through.
And the fierce Christ,
Split, shaken free,
Flings up, rejoicing,
Upswung, outflung,
Larklike released,
Climbs skyward,
Hovers at the lightning's tip.
And over all the earth
Drops down the plenitudinous
Great gain, the torrential

Rains of that release.
For the great side splits.
The packed incarnate Blood
Pours to the world's black womb
The funnelling Seed.
Idea and Instinct
Fuse on the stroke of Three,
The sear and shuddering strike
That makes all be.

Storm whines.
The rent Christ-body
Flaps like an empty sack
Upon the Tree.

◆

Thou art come.

Up from the desert,
Flowing with delights,
Thou didst lean upon Thy beloved.

In the springtime of the night
I felt in my flesh
Thy sudden hand.

Thou hast put Thy hand through the hole in the door.
My womb was moved at Thy touch.

I have entered.
Thou hast gone up into the palm tree
And taken the fruits thereof.
Thou hast made me known.

As that Seal upon Thy arm.
As that Sign upon Thy heart.
Thy hand
Strong as death;
Thy mouth
Hard as hell.
And the lamps of flames and fire.

I know Thee, God
As Thou, God, knowest Thy own.

What hast Thou done to Thy sister
In the day that she was spoken to?

My womb is awake.
Thou hast breathed in my belly
And made a bourning there.

I am breached.

If I be a wall
Build on me Thy bulwark of silver.
If I be a door
Join me with Thy cedar boards.
There is no more death.

My breasts are as a tower. I am
Become in Thy presence
As one finding peace.

I am grown great.
Thou hast made a birth in me, God.
I am wombed of a wonder.

It was time and past time.

The vineyard was before Thee,
Thou hast crowded in.

I am grown good.
My perfect one
Is but one.

God knows me.
            In me
God knows and needs nothing,
Who is.
        In Thee, God,
I am Thou.
            O sola
Beatitude!
            My soul,
God's womb, is seeded
Of God's own.
            My womb,
God's own, is sown

Of God's seed.
             My soul,
Wombed of God's wonder,
Is seeded, sown.

Thou that dwellest in the Gardens
Make me hear Thy voice.

Christ-crossed I bleed.

I am One.

A Canticle to the Christ in the Holy Eucharist

Written on the Feast of St. Therese of the Child Jesus,
Virgin and Contemplative, 1953.

Gustate, et videte quoniam suavis est Dominus!
—PSALM XXXIII

And the many days and the many nights that I lay as one barren,
As the barren doe lies on in the laurel under the slope of Mt.
    Tamalpais,
The fallow doe in the deep madrone, in the tall grove of the redwoods,
Curling her knees on the moist earth where the spring died out of the
    mountain.
Her udder is dry. Her dugs are dry as the fallen leaves of the laurel,
Where she keeps her bed in the laurel clump on the slope of Tamalpais.

Sudden as wind that breaks east out of dawn this morning you struck,
As wind that poured from the wound of dawn in the valley of my
    beginning.
Your look rang like the strident quail, like the buck that stamps in the
    thicket.
Your face was the flame. Your mouth was the rinse of wine. Your
    tongue, the torrent.

I fed on that terror as hunger is stanched on meat, the taste and the
    trembling.
In the pang of my dread you smiled and swept to my heart.
As the eagle eats so I ate, as the hawk takes flesh from his talon,
As the mountain lion clings and kills, I clung and was killed.

This kill was thy name. In the wound of my heart thy voice was the
    cling,
Like honey out of the broken rock thy name and the stroke of thy kiss.
The heart wound and the hovering kiss they looked to each other,
As the lovers gaze in their clasp, the grave embrace of love.

This name and the wound of my heart partook of each other.
They had no use but to feed, the grazing of love.
Thy name and the gaze of my heart they made one wound together.
This wound-made-one was their thought, the means of their
    knowledge.

There is nothing known like this wound, this knowledge of love.
In what love? In which wounds, such words? In what touch? In whose
    coming?
You gazed. Like the voice of the quail. Like the buck that stamps in the
    thicket.
You gave. You found the gulf, the goal. On my tongue you were meek.

In my heart you were might. And thy word was the running of rain
That rinses October. And the sweetwater spring in the rock. And the
    brook in the crevice.
Thy word in my heart was the start of the buck that is sourced in the
    doe.
Thy word was the milk that will be in her dugs, the stir of new life
    in them.
You gazed. I stood barren for days, lay fallow for nights.
Thy look was the movement of life, the milk in the young breasts
    of mothers.

My mouth was the babe's. You had stamped like the buck in the
manzanita.
My heart was dry as the dugs of the doe in the fall of the year on
Tamalpais.
I sucked thy wound as the fawn sucks milk from the crowning breast of
its mother.
The flow of thy voice in my shrunken heart was the cling of wild honey,
The honey that bled from the broken comb in the cleft of Tamalpais.

The quick of thy kiss lives on in my heart with the strike, the wound
you inflicted,
Like the print of the hind feet of the buck in the earth of Tamalpais.
You left thy look like a blaze on my heart, the sudden gash in the
granite,
The blow that broke the honeycomb in the rock of Tamalpais.

And the blaze of the buck is left in the doe, his seal that none may have
her.
She is bred. She takes his sign to the laurel clump, and will not be seen.
She will lie under laurel and never be seen. She will keep his secret.
She will guard in her womb his planted pang. She will prove her token.
She will hold the sign that set her trust, the seal of her communion.

I will feed thy kiss: as the doe seeks out the laurel clump and feeds her
treasure.
I will nurse in my heart the wound you made, the gash of thy delivery.
I will bear that blaze in my struck soul, in my body bring it.
It keeps in me now as the sign in the doe, the new life in the mother.

For each in that wound is each, and quick is quick, and we gaze,
A look that lives unslaked in the wound that it inflicted.
My gaze and thine, thy gaze and mine, in these the troth is taken.
The double gaze and the double name in the sign of the quenchless
    wound,
The wound that throbs like wakening milk in the winter dugs of the
    doe,
Like honey out of the broken comb in the rock of Tamalpais.

Thou art gone. I will keep the wound till you show. I will wait in the
    laurel.
I know as the knowledge is of the doe where she lies on Tamalpais.
In the deep madrone. In the oak. In the tall grove of the redwoods.
Where she lies in laurel and proves the wound on the slope of Mt.
    Tamalpais.

The South Coast

Salt creek mouths unflushed by the sea
And the long day shuts down.
Whose hand stacks rock, cairn-posted,
Churched to the folded sole of this hill,
And Whose mind conceives? Three herons
Gig their necks in the tule brake
And the prying mud hen plies.
Long down, far south to Sur, the wind lags,
Slosh-washes his slow heel,
Lays off our coast, rump of the domed
Mountain, woman-backed, bedded
Under his lee. Salt grasses here,
Fringes, twigging the crevice slips,
And the gagging cypress
Wracked away from the sea.
God *makes*. On earth, in us, most instantly,
On the very now,
His own means conceives.
How many strengths break out unchoked
Where He, Whom all declares,
Delights to make be!

Annul in Me My Manhood

The Lord gives these favors far more to women than to men; I have heard the saintly Fray Peter of Alcantara say that, and I have observed it myself. He would say that women made much more progress on this road than men, and gave excellent reasons for this, which there is no point in my repeating here, all in favor of women.
     — ST. TERESA OF AVILA

Annul in me my manhood, Lord, and make
Me woman-sexed and weak,
If by that total transformation
I might know Thee more.
What is the worth of my own sex
That the bold possessive instinct
Should but shoulder Thee aside?
What uselessness is housed in my loins,
To drive, drive, the rampant pride of life,
When what is needful is a hushed quiescence?
"The soul is feminine to God,"
And hangs on impregnation,
Fertile influxing Grace. But how achieve
The elemental lapse of that repose,
That watchful, all-abiding silence of the soul,
In which the Lover enters to His own,
Yielding Himself to her, and her alone?
How may a man assume that hiddenness of heart
Being male, all masculine and male,
Blunt with male hunger?

                    Make me then
Girl-hearted, virgin-souled, woman-docile, maiden-meek;
Cancel in me the rude compulsive tide
That like an angry river surges through,
Flouts off Thy soft lip-touches, froth-blinds
The soul-gaze from its very great delight,
Outbawls the rare celestial melody.
Restless I churn. The use of sex is union,
Union alone. Here it but cleaves,
Makes man the futile ape of God, all ape
And no bride, usurps the energizing role, inverts;
And in that wrenched inversion caught
Draws off the needer from his never-ending need, diverts
The seeker from the Sought.

Out of the Ash

Solstice of the dark, the absolute
Zero of the year. Praise God
Who comes for us again, our lives
Pulled to their fisted knot,
Cinched tight with cold, drawn
To the heart's constriction; our faces
Seamed like clinkers in the grate,
Hands like tongs—Praise God
That Christ, phoenix immortal,
Springs up again from solstice ash,
Drives his equatorial ray
Into our cloud, emblazons
Our stiff brow, fries
Our chill tears. Come Christ,
Most gentle and throat-pulsing Bird!
O come, sweet Child! Be gladness
In our church! Waken with anthems
Our bare rafters! O phoenix
Forever! Virgin-wombed
And burning in the dark,
Be born! Be born!

River-Root: A Syzygy

River-Root: as even under high drifts, those fierce wind-grappled cuts
    of the Rockies,
One listening will hear, far down below, the softest seepage, a new
    melt, a faint draining,
And know for certain that this is the tip, this, though the leastest trace,
Is indeed the uttermost inch of the River.

Or on cloud-huddled days up there shut in white denseness,
Where peaks in that blindness call back and forth each to the other,
Skim but a finger along a twig, slick off the moist,
A mere dampness the cloud has left, a vague wetness.
But still you know this too is a taking, this too can be sea,
The active element, pure inception, the residual root of the River.

Place a hand under moss, brush back a fern, turn over a stone, scoop
    out a hollow—
Is there already, the merest wet, the least moistness, and is enough—
No more than this is needful for source,
So much is a start, such too makes up the rise of the River.

Even this, even these, of little more, of nothing less,
Of each, of all, drop and by drop, the very coolness priming the wind
Alone suffices: this in itself, for all its slightness, can birth the River.

And hence such wetness gains liquid body and cups a spring,
Lipped down from a crevice, some stone-slotted vein of the mauled
    mountain,
A jet of liberation, and in so much is swiftly away.
And the spurt makes a trickle, channelling out an edge for itself,
Forming a bed of itself as it goes, a bottom of gravel.

Two join together, they find a third, the fourth sucks in making a fifth.
One and by one, down crick, over bar, under bush, beyond bend,
They merge and they melt, they start and they stretch.
The frozen glaciers fuse and further, the long high levels give up their
    gifts.

And now over all the rock-walls the River sweeps, he stoops and
    plunges.
He has found his scope and is on his way.
Let slopes drop slides, let ponderosas topple athwart him—
Log jams of winter, storm-sundered roots and the breakage of forests
Clog up canyons—for him these are nothing.

He has found his strength and takes no defection.
He has smelled his term in his prime beginning and will not be fended.
He carries sea in his gut: heels in the peaks but his throat at the Gulf;
Spending is all he knows.

Spending, to spend, his whole libido: to spend is his sex.

For the River is male. He is raking down ridges,
And sucks up mud from alluvial flats, far muck-bottomed valleys.

He drags cold silt a long way, a passion to bring,
Keeps reaching back for what he has left and channelling on.
All head: but nonetheless his roots are restless.
They have need of suckling, the passion to fulfill. In the glut of hunger
He chews down the kneecaps of mountains.

And bringing down to bring on has but one resolve: to deliver.
It is this that makes up his elemental need,
Constitutes his primal ground, the under-aching sex of the River.

For deep in his groin he carries the fore-thrusting phallos of his might
That sucks up a continent, pouring it into the sea.
A passion for elseness lurks in his root. As the father in child-getting
Draws back on his body, the furthermost nerves of his great
      physique—
Beyond the root phallos and the slumberous reservoirs of his seed,
Far up the tall spinal range of his torso, the mountainous back and the
      cloud-hung shoulders,
Above the interlinking neck to the high domed summit, the somnolent
      skull,
Those uttermost lakes of the brimming brain—so does the river-
      phallos draw on the land.

Out of the fields and forests, out of the cornland and cottonland,
Out of the buttes and measureless prairies, out of high ridges, the
      remotest mountains,
Out of the gut, the taut belly and smouldering lava-filled loins of the
      continent,
The male god draws, serpentine giant, phallic thrust and vengeance,
The sex-enduring, life-bestowing, father of waters: the River.

Flying over at dusk on a clear day, trending across it
Coiled below, a shimmer of light, sinuous, the quicksilver runner,
Deep-linking nerve of the vast continent, a sleeping snake.
You follow it down as the light fails, massive, majestic,
Thick and inert, recumbent, torpid with sentient power.

Slowly night takes it. When darkness drops on the valley
The River, iridescent, beats on through hot clay,
Its need and its passion dreaming far forward a full thousand miles:
Its head in the uterine sea.

For the strong long River
Leaps to the Gulf, earth-lover, broacher, dredger of female silt and
     engorger, sperm-thruster.
And behind all its maleness that mulling might.
The gnawn rockheads jut for peaks, ridgepoles of height,
Where fork-lightning splices flicked roots in heaven,
Tall sap-swollen trees thrust juice at the sky,
Murmurous with pollen, their potent musk.

And the high cut crags.
There bighorn ram covers his ewe in a rushing tussle, the loose rock
Swirls under chipping hooves; it falls a thousand feet: when it hits
Fire flashes below.

And the water-delled flats.
The mountain buck springs his start in the doe,
Pine-needled earth rucked under his pitch, the rubbed antlers rattling.
And balsam barrens where the grizzly, sullen, roused to slow joy,
Mauls his fierce woman crazed with desire.

And lily-pad lakes where the bull moose thrashes his scoop-sweep
    head,
The huge horns flailing. In the throes of his mate-move
Tramples shallows, cattails shatter, the black testes swinging. His love
Dredges up sperm, souse of his juice streaking her belly,
Seed-rush to the womb.

And those everlasting plains where the buffalo bull couples his cow,
Massive, the humped mountainous shoulders, domed primordial hulk
    of his head
Reared skyward, that ponderous love.

And the randy squirrel, the scuttling rabbit,
Lolling coyote, the prancing pronghorn.

Out of the teeming maleness of earth the black River plunges.

And over his length streaked birds dip down, sip water up in their
    parching beaks,
Stagger-winged skimmers: slaked they fly on.
The beating drake, the honking gander, their necks
Arched in splendor, gabbling under the mating moon,
Knife-blade wings in that watery couple
Slashing torn reeds, a thrash of pinions. They tread down the bitten
Half-drowned heads of shy hens, a mighty thunder.
They wade through flat water.

                    And the fecund fish:
Great pikes in their plunge, each trailing his mate:
Quick trout dartling glib river-shallows.

Deep down under
The snapping turtle sulks in his cutbank hole. Over his head
Bigmouth bass break water for joy. Far back on the bayou
One bull frog swells his organ-note gong: the syllable of desire
Booms over the bog.

And the River runs.

Passion Week

Christ-cut: the cedar
Bleeds where I gashed it.

Lance wound under the narrow rib.

Eve's orifice: the agony of Abel
Enacted out on the Tree.

Blood gushed
From the gash.

The Holy Ghost
Gusted out of the sky
Aghast.

Our Guest.

Bleed cedar.
Little cedar,
Lanced,
Axe-opened,
The ache of sacrifice.

Pour out,
As Christ,
Those pearls of pain,
Bequeathed.

O bleed
Little cedar,
Bleed for the blooded Heart,
For the pang of man . . .

The earth's
Old ache.

You, God

A land of darkness, and of the shadow of death,
without any order, where the light is as darkness.
— THE BOOK OF JOB

Nor any day gone,
Nor any night,
Measureless over the rimrock.

Nor those black imaginary suns
Roaring under the earth,
Roasting the roots of trees.

If I beg death, God, it is of you.

If I seize life, it is out of you.
If I lose, if I lose,
It is unto you.

God of death,
Great God of no-life,
Existence is mine,
But you
Broach a nothingness
Breached out of nowhere.

Always you are not yet.

Deep in my guts,
Choked on oblivion,
Split, hearted on annihilation,
Caught through,
Smothered out,
A terror of emptiness,
Spat.

Immutable silence
Enormous over the snow mesa,
Enormous over the lava crag,
The wind-worked cloud.

My brain
Burns on your pierce.
My blood splits.
I shriek each nerve.

God!

Suck me in!

A Frost Lay White on California

Thou shalt not offer the hire of a strumpet, nor the price
of a dog, in the house of the Lord thy God, whatsoever
it be that thou hast vowed: because both these are an
abomination to the Lord thy God.

—THE BOOK OF DEUTERONOMY

God. Spell dawns
Drained of all light.
Spell the masterhood of the means,
The flanges of extinction.
Spell the impotence of the numbed mouth,
Hurt, clenched on the bone of repudiation,
Spurning.

I grind it down. I grind on it.
I have yet to eat it up.

Crouched in my choir stall,
My heart fisted on stubborn revolt,
My two arms crossed on my chest,
Braced there, the cloak
Swaddling me round.

It is night.
I bore the darkness with my eyes,
Tearing it up.

Over the chapel the cold
Snaps on the roof,
Ringing with silence.
Two hours, spanning two inches of darkness.
I feel stars like hoarfrost prickle the tallness.
There ought to be a dawn.

"Do you think, O man, in that high
Toss of desire, that sheer
Aspirative hanker of yours,
What deeps go unplumbed?
Something within you is grinding its axle,
Spitting out sparks.
Stop for one moment,
Or ever so little,
And be assured you have read it aright.
That which is written between those flanges,
Spelled on the walls of the vascular heart,
Is your own scrawl.
What scars have you gouged on the stone of that cave?"

Fingered down in my deeps, I deny it.
What desolation, that depth!
Who says so!
What secret, that scrivening!
My own business, you.
Leave me alone.

"Do you think," cried God, "to have spat in my face
Driving me off that easily?

I ask you nothing not accorded a dog:
One glance of recognition.
To own what I am.
Which is you.
I am your image!"

The dark held through.
The stars, frozen, spit seeds in the sky.
I thought giant Orion,
The club-tossed arm,
Hurls over the house.
At ground level the frost
Gnawed at, bit tree-trash,
Loose leaf-stuff.

"I will not quit you," cried God, "for we are inseparable!
Do you hear? My name
Is carved on your heart,
There among the graffiti,
In capital letters.
That is my gash,
The struck brand,
The wound you made in your violence.
It will never heal.
You do not know how much I am you:
The other side of your face,
The back side of your body.
I stand between your shoulders.
I am that void behind your eyes
When you can't think!"

I wondered about the dawn, where it could be.
I sensed the wind veer south and west.
Two days it had held
To die in that quarter.
And in such death, out of that clear, frost fell.
Now the choir
Hung black and empty,
Hell's belly.
I felt the new wind, south,
Grope her tonguing mouth on the wall.
What does she want, this woman-wind?
She is trying to rain.

"Never forget," cried God, "I am your slave!
Call me and I come.
Curse me, I cannot quit.
I have never renounced.
Do you know what I am?
I am your woman.
That is my mouth you feel on your heart,
Breathing there, warming it.
I am more. I am your dog.
That is my moan you hear in your blood,
The ache of the dog for the master.
I am your dog-woman.
I grieve a man down,
Moan till he melts."

There was a rustling of winter-scarred weeds in the gutter.
It was winter, midwinter.
It was night, midnight, past midnight.
It was the dawn night. The scars in my heart
Were gashed by a terrible hand.
I clenched my heart on that gash.
I cursed.

"You are of flesh," cried God, "that is your light!
The shimmering sensitivity of the nerve.
Not I!
No brain to think with!
No nerve to think through!
I am dog in that I follow,
Woman in that I love.
Seek me!
In the heart of your disgust,
The germ of your revulsion,
The glint of truth impacted in your terror.
Invade me!
Flee that Luciferian
Light of the brain,
Pride of your life!
Down! Down! Behind! Below!
Quick! I am gone!
I, woman, moan against the bars.
I, dog, bay against the dawn."

I raised my head.
On such a night, long ago, when I was a boy,
There would have been a rooster
To rip the silence with a murderous yell.
I heard the wind turn west, southwest.
I said to myself: Do you think it will rain?

"Do you want it to," cried God, "and what for?
This ground is frozen.
Frost has locked hard on it now for too long.
The seeds are all tight.
Their lips are sealed.
They wonder when it will come a change.
They are like you."

I jerked back my hood,
Fighting the ache of my bones.
I am a fool.
Birds stirred out there in the crotches of bushes.
What red-breasted linnet will throat that dawn,
His voice a thorn?

"I have nothing to conceal," cried God, "from those deeps of your
passion!
Why should I lie?
Read your own hate if you would know.
Would I squander blood on such as you if I didn't mean it?
Bah! I am always in earnest.
My hunger is plain as the pang in your gut.
Feed me! I am you!"

Was this a dream,
Some phantasy of anguish?
I crouched in my stall all night.
It was winter, midwinter.
A frost lay white on California.
I felt stars crack blue in my brain.

"I ask nothing," cried God, "that you wouldn't accord a dog!
I told you that!
The sheerest recognition.
That I do exist.
That I am yours.
Close your eyes now and be what I am.
Which is—yourself!
The you who am I!"

The roof of the chapel split up the sky,
A tree-wedge in a stump.
I felt the cold stitch my bones.
I should be in bed.
This is a fool to knock about here in the frozen hour,
Champing my teeth like a chittering ghost.
Who do I think I am?

"Who, indeed," cried God, "when you think what you think?
Ask me who, I will tell it!
How far do I have to go?
Look! I crawl at your feet!
I, the God-dog!
I am all woman!

I eat from your hand!
Feed me. All I ask is your heart.
Am I that ugly?"

The light woke in the windows.
One by one the saints existed,
The swords of their martyrdom healed in their hands.
The linnet opened his voice;
He blistered his throat on the seethe of that rapture.
The suddenness split my skull.

"No pride!" cried God, "kick me I come back!
Spit on me I eat your spittle!
I crawl on my belly!
When you have gutted this madness
Drop down on the ground.
I will lick your hand."

That was the moment the dawn dragged in,
The cloud closed. It had slid from the sea,
Almost a sneak. I stood up in my stall,
Flung off my cloak. I heard the rain begin.

It was falling on the roof,
A slow spilth of deliverance,
Falling far, very far.

It was falling, I knew, out of the terrifying helplessness of God.

Into the frost,
Into the frozen crotches of the bush,
Into the feather of the singing bird.

Across the stuttering mouths of those seeds;
Against the sob of my tongue.

I Am Long Weaned

When I looked for good then evil came, and when I waited for light then came darkness. My bowels boil, and rest not.
— THE BOOK OF JOB

I am long weaned.

My mouth, puckered on gall,
Sucks dry curd.

My thoughts, those sterile watercourses
Scarring a desert.

My throat is lean meat.
In my belly no substance is,
Nor water moves.

My gut goes down
A straight drop to my groin.

My cod is withered string,
My seed, two flints in a sack.

Some day, in some other place,
Will come a rain;
Will come water out of deep wells,
Will come melons sweet from the vine.

I will know God.

Sophia, deep wisdom,
The splendid unquenchable fount:

Unbind those breasts.

In the Breach

God!

The I-killer!
The me-death!

Rip me out!

Crouched in my womb,
Reality-butting head,
Mute-mouthed,
Gagged.

Breach!

Head-hunched,
Pelvis-pulled,
Heel-seized,
Sky-swung.

God!

My first scream
Skewers all night.
Far down
Earth's groan,

Gripe-gout,
The mother-grunt,
Gasps.

Where I?

God!

Caul-freed
I cry!

In All These Acts

Cleave the wood and thou shalt find Me, lift the rock
and I am there!
— THE GOSPEL ACCORDING TO THOMAS

Dawn cried out: the brutal voice of a bird
Flattened the seaglaze. Treading that surf
Hunch-headed fishers toed small agates,
Their delicate legs, iridescent, stilting the ripples.
Suddenly the cloud closed. They heard big wind
Boom back on the cliff, crunch timber over along the ridge.
They shook up their wings, crying; terror flustered their pinions.
Then hemlock, tall, torn by the roots, went crazily down,
The staggering gyrations of splintered kindling.
Flung out of bracken, fleet mule deer bolted;
But the great elk, caught midway between two scissoring logs,
Arched belly-up and died, the snapped spine
Half torn out of his peeled back, his hind legs
Jerking that gasped convulsion, the kick of spasmed life,
Paunch plowed open, purple entrails
Disgorged from the basketwork ribs
Erupting out, splashed sideways, wrapping him,
Gouted in blood, flecked with the brittle sliver of bone.
Frenzied, the terrible head
Thrashed off its antlered fuzz in that rubble
And then fell still, the great tongue
That had bugled in rut, calling the cow-elk up from the glades,
Thrust agonized out, the maimed member
Bloodily stiff in the stone-smashed teeth . . .

                                        Far down below,
The mountain torrent, that once having started
Could never be stopped, scooped up that avalanchial wrack
And strung it along, a riddle of bubble and littered duff
Spun down its thread. At the gorged river mouth
The sea plunged violently in, gasping its potholes,
Sucked and panted, answering itself in its spume.
The river, spent at last, beating driftwood up and down
In a frenzy of capitulation, pumped out its life,
Destroying itself in the mother sea,
There where the mammoth sea-grown salmon
Lurk immemorial, roe in their hulls, about to begin.
They will beat that barbarous beauty out
On those high-stacked shallows, those headwater claims,
Back where they were born. Along that upward-racing trek
Time springs through all its loops and flanges,
The many-faced splendor and the music of the leaf,
The copulation of beasts and the watery laughter of drakes,
Too few the grave witnesses, the wakeful, vengeful beauty,
Devolving itself of its whole constraint,
Erupting as it goes.

                    In all these acts
Christ crouches and seethes, pitched forward
On the crucifying stroke, juvescent, that will spring Him
Out of the germ, out of the belly of the dying buck,
Out of the father-phallus and the torn-up root.
These are the modes of His forth-showing,
His serene agonization. In the clicking teeth of otters

Over and over He dies and is born,
Shaping the weasel's jaw in His leap
And the staggering rush of the bass.

God Germed in Raw Granite

God germed in raw granite, source-glimpsed in stone?
Or imaged out in the black-flamed
Onyx-open line, smoldered in the tortured
Free-flow of lava, the igneous
Instant of conception? As maiden-form
Swells in the heaviness of wold, sleeps
Rumped and wanton-bulged in the boulder's
Bulk, is shaped in tree-forms everywhere
As any may see: dropped logs, say, or those crotched
Trunks pronged like a reckless nymph
Head-plunged into the earth—so Godhood
Wakes under water, shape-lurked, or grave and somber,
Where sea falls, mocks through flung foam . . .

                                       Ghost!
Can this be? Breather of elemental truths,
She stirs, she coaxes! Out of my heart's howk,
Out of my soul's wild wrath
I make oath! In my emptiness
These arms gall for her, bride's mouth,
Spent-breathed in laughter, or that night's
First unblushing revealment, the flexed
Probity of the flesh, the hymen-hilted troth,
We closed, we clung on it, the stroked
And clangorous rapture!

I am dazed.
Is this she? Woman within!
Can this be? Do we, His images, float
Time-spun on that vaster drag
His timelessness evokes?
In the blind heart's core, when we,
Well-wedded merge, by Him
Twained into one and solved there,
Are these still three? Are three
So oned, in the full-forthing
(Heart's reft, the spirit's great
Unreckonable grope, and God's
Devouring splendor in the stroke) are we—
This all, this utterness, this terrible
Total truth—indubitably He?

The Song the Body Dreamed
in the Spirit's Mad Behest

I am black but beautiful, O ye daughters of Jerusalem.
Look not upon me because I am black, because the Sun
has looked upon me.
— THE SONG OF SONGS

The Imagination, unable to grasp the reality of pure
Spirit, conceives of their union under the modality of
her own nature. Longing to respond totally to the di-
vine summons, and convinced in faith that the Re-
demption has rendered this possible, she struggles to
cast off all the inhibitions of original sin, and evokes
the deepest resources of her sensuality, in order to
achieve in shamelessness the wholeness of being an
age of shame has rendered incomplete.

Call Him the Lover and call me the Bride.
Lapsing upon the couch of His repose
I heard the elemental waters rise,
Divide, and close.

I heard Him tremble and I turned my head.
Behold, the pitiless fondness of His eyes;
Dark, the rapacious terror of the heart
In orgy cries.

His eyes upon me wanton into life
What has slept long and never known the surge;
Bequeath an excess spilt of the blood's delight,
And the heart's purge.

His lips have garnished fruits out of my breast
That maddens Him to forage on my throat,
Moan against my dread the finite pang
Of the soul's gloat.

He is the Spirit but I am the Flesh.
Out of my body must He be reborn,
Soul from the sundered soul, Creation's gout
In the world's bourn.

Mounted between the thermals of my thighs
Hawklike He hovers surging at the sun,
And feathers me a frenzy ringed around
That deep drunk tongue.

The Seal is broken and the Blood is gushed.
He does not check but boldens in His pace.
The fierce mouth has beaked out both my eyes,
And signed my face.

His tidal strength within me shores and brunts,
The ooze of oil, the slaver of the bitch,
The bull's gore, the stallion's famished gnash,
And the snake's itch.

Grit of great rivers boasting to the sea,
Geysers in spume, islands that leveled lie,
One snow-peak agonized against the bleak
Inviolate sky.

Folding Him in the chaos of my loins
I pierce through armies tossed upon my breast,
Envelop in love's tidal dredge of faith
His huge unrest.

But drifting into depth that what might cease
May be prolonged until a night is lost,
We starve the splendor lapsing in the loins,
Curb its great cost.

Mouthless we grope for meaning in that void
That melds between us from our listening blood,
While passion throbs the chopped cacophony
Of our strange good.

Proving what instinct sobs of total quest
When shapeless thunder stretches into life,
And the Spirit, bleeding, rears to overreach
The buttocks' strife.

That will be how we lose what we have gained,
The incremental rapture at the core,
Spleened of the belly's thick placental wrath,
And the seed's roar.

Born and reborn we will be groped, be clenched
On ecstasies that shudder toward crude birth,
When His great Godhead peels its stripping strength
In my red earth.

The Poet Is Dead

A Memorial for Robinson Jeffers

To be read with a full stop between
the strophes, as in a dirge.

In the evening the dusk
Stipples with lights. The long shore
Gathers darkness in on itself
And goes cold. From the lap of silence
All the tide-crest's pivotal immensity
Lifts into the land.

◆

Snow on the headland,
Rare on the coast of California.
Snow on Point Lobos,
Falling all night,
Filling the creeks and the back country,
The strangely beautiful
Setting of death.

◆

For the poet is dead.
The pen, splintered on the sheer
Excesses of vision, unfingered, falls.
The heart-crookt hand, cold as a stone,
Lets it go down.

◆

The great tongue is dried.
The teeth that bit to the bitterness
Are sheathed in truth.

♦

If you listen
You can hear the field mice
Kick little rifts in the snow-swirls.
You can hear
Time take back its own.

♦

For the poet is dead.
On the bed by the window,
Where dislike and desire
Killed each other in the crystalline interest,
What remains alone lets go of its light. It has found
Finalness. It has touched what it craved: the passionate
Darks of deliverance.

♦

At sundown the sea wind,
Burgeoning,
Bled the west empty.

♦

Now the opulent
Treacherous woman called Life
Forsakes her claim. Blond and a harlot
She once drank joy from his narrow loins.
She broke his virtue in her knees.

♦

In the water-gnawn coves of Point Lobos
The white-faced sea otters
Fold their paws on their velvet breasts
And list waveward.

♦

But he healed his pain on the wisdom of stone.
He touched roots for his peace.

♦

For the poet is dead. The gaunt wolf
Crawled out to the edge and died snapping.
He said he would. The wolf
Who lost his mate. He said he would carry the wound,
The blood-wound of life, to the broken edge
And die grinning.

♦

Over the salt marsh the killdeer,
Unrestrainable,
Cry fear against moonset.

♦

And all the hardly suspected
Latencies of disintegration
Inch forward. The skin
Flakes loss. On the death-gripped feet
The toenails glint like eyeteeth
From the pinched flesh.
The caged ribs and the bladed shoulders,
Ancient slopes of containment,
Imperceptibly define the shelves of structure,

Faced like rock ridges
Boned out of mountains, absently revealed
With the going of the snow.

♦

In the sleeve of darkness the gopher
Tunnels the sod for short grass
And pockets his fill.

♦

And the great phallus shrinks in the groin,
The seed in the scrotum
Chills.

♦

When the dawn comes in again,
Thoughtlessly,
The sea birds will mew by the window.

♦

For the poet is dead. Beyond the courtyard
The ocean at full tide hunches its bulk.
Groping among the out-thrusts of granite
It moans and whimpers. In the phosphorescent
Restlessness it chunks deceptively,
Wagging its torn appendages, dipping and rinsing
Its ripped sea rags, its strip-weeded kelp.
The old mother grieves her deathling.
She trundles the dark for her lost child.
She hunts her son.

♦

On the top of the tower
The hawk will not perch tomorrow.

   ◆

But in the gorged rivermouth
Already the steelhead fight for entry.
They feel fresh water
Sting through the sieves of their salt-coarsened gills.
They shudder and thrust.

   ◆

So the sea broods. And the aged gull,
Asleep on the water, too stiff to feed,
Spins in a side-rip crossing the surf
And drags down.

   ◆

This mouth is shut. I say
The mouth is clamped cold.
I tell you this tongue is dried.

   ◆

But the skull, the skull,
The perfect sculpture of bone! —
Around the forehead the fine hair,
Composed to the severest
Lineaments of thought,
Is moulded on peace.

   ◆

And the strongly-wrought features,
That keep in the soul's serenest achievement
The spirit's virtue,

Set the death mask of all mortality,
The impress of that grace.

◆

In the shoal-champed breakers
One wing of the gull
Tilts like a fin through the ribbon of spume
And knifes under.

◆

And all about there the vastness of night
Affirms its sovereignty. There's not a cliff
Of the coastline, not a reef
Of the waterways, from the sword-thrust Aleutians
To the scorpion-tailed stinger Cape Horn—
All that staggering declivity
Grasped in the visionary mind and established—
But is sunken under the dark ordainment,
Like a sleeper possessed, like a man
Gone under, like a powerful swimmer
Plunged in a womb-death washed out to sea
And worked back ashore.

◆

The gull's eye,
Skinned to the wave, retains the ocean's
Imponderable compression,
And burns yellow.

◆

The poet is dead. I tell you
The nostrils are narrowed. I say again and again
The strong tongue is broken.

◆

But the owl
Quirks in the cypresses, and you hear
What he says. He is calling for something.
He tucks his head for his mate's
Immemorial whisper. In her answering voice
He tastes the grace-note of his reprieve.

◆

When fog comes again to the canyons
The redwoods will know what it means.
The giant sisters
Gather it into their merciful arms
And stroke silence.

◆

You smell pine resin laced in the salt
And know the dawn wind has veered.

◆

And on the shelf in the gloom,
Blended together, the tall books emerge,
All of a piece. Transparent as membranes
The thin leaves of paper hug their dark thoughts.
They know what he said.

◆

The sea, reaching for life,
Spits up the gull. He falls spread-eagled,
The streaked wings swept on the sand.
Vague fingers of snow, aimlessly deft, grope for his eyes.
When the blind head snaps
The beak krakes at the sky.

♦

Now the night closes.
All the dark's negatory
Decentralization
Quivers toward dawn.

♦

He has gone into death like a stone thrown in the sea.

♦

And in far places the morning
Shrills its episodes of triviality and vice
And one man's passing. Could the ears
That hardly listened in life
Care much less now?

♦

Snow on the headland,
The strangely beautiful
Oblique concurrence,
The strangely beautiful
Setting of death.

♦

The great tongue
Dries in the mouth. I told you.
The voiceless throat
Cools silence. And the sea-granite eyes.
Washed in the sibilant waters
The stretched lips kiss peace.

♦

The poet is dead.

♦

Nor will ever again hear the sea lions
Grunt in the kelp at Point Lobos.
Nor look to the south when the grunion
Run the Pacific, and the plunging
Shearwaters, insatiable,
Stun themselves in the sea.

The Kiss of the Cross

I

I cry.

Once of this world,
Woman of God,
What do you betoken?

Heart of fire,
Violence of flesh,
The spirit's flash,
Voice of tolled desire.

Tongue of wrath,
Latencies, the fierce
Evocation: semblances,
The shut darkness broken.

Over the bay
City-light wavers and spurns.
One steamer
Sidles the mist,
Homes the black harbor.

Pound heart,
Heart of the splendored rapture,
Ruptured on death.

In the trace of a hand,
On the mystery of a face
The brute heart is shaken.

II

The heart reaves: my flesh
Coughs from its clotted need,
One flex of possession.

All flung pride
Crashes on that crest.

Her face reels,
God's voice blares.

The crucifix
Snaps.

In the tongs of passion
Is torn,
Is torn.

Let the heart be hit
If ever it can.
Let the bludgeoned soul
Stone its mute mouth.

In the outreach of love,
In the passion of possession,
I nailed my desire.

III

Heart be hushed.
Let it howk and then hush.

Let the black wave break.
Let the terrible tongue
Engorge my deeps.

Let the loins of ferocity
Lave my shut flesh.

I killed the Christ.

On the inch of my pride,
On the diamond of my desire,
In the pierce of a woman's goodness,
By the token of her grace.

I who crept toward him year after year
Murdered my God.

IV

I crept.

I brought Him gifts,
Hushed in my heart.

I brought what I had.

I crept.

I gave Him every gift of myself.
I brought Him all the wholeness I had.

V

I brought Him my wholeness,
That wholeness was split.

I brought Him my burden,
That burden broke.

I brought Him my all,
My all was empty.

In the wrath of flesh
I heard His bone
Snap like a nerve.

My passion poured.

VI

My passion poured.

I heard His nerve
Snap like a bone.

135

I came:
    up out of darkness,
    deep holes and recesses,
    black wells and cisterns of the self—
I came!
I came!

I cried my pang!
The burden
Split bone in the dark!

He shrieked.

As I gasped
He fell dead.

I panted across her face
Feeling Him bleed.

I saw her kneel.
She kissed His cross.

    VII

She kissed.
My shame charred my face.
With her voice she consoled.
In her mother-hands
She knitted His bones.

When she kissed His knees
His face smiled.

I thrashed in that dark
Strangled with guilt.

What deeds of wrath from the spilt gift!

Shameful the face of the shocked man
Who wept in my place.

I spit heart's blood.
My fist a claw
Scrabbled my heart.

She kissed.
I saw Him sag.

That dark was dead.

VIII

She kissed.

With her lips she consoled.
My soul shook.

I screeched back in dread.

As a cool water flows
Her words were.

I saw stars steeped in death over San Francisco.

Her words:
She gave up a song that a heart might heal.
I flinched on her prayer.
Picking my sin like a stone out of dirt
I bore it home.

I held it against my raddled groin,
My jewel of pain on which Christ died.

While I slept it burned on.

IX

While I slept it burned.
A stone in my bed it lay nightlong,
A passion to purge me.

In my mirror of death
Her face sustained me.

In my substance of guilt
Her purity betrayed me.

I slashed with my seed.

She bore the flesh-wound under the breast,
The mother-burden.

By the kissed cross,
Where the Christ-nerve

Snapped when my passion poured,
Clinched on the Tree:

She brought me back.

    x

She brought me back.
The kiss that kept me:

A heart to heal,
A death to die,
The debt of a death.

I was brought back alive.

Drenched in that deed when passion poured,
Her purity betrayed me.

Merciless that armor
Turned the point of my brutal tongue.

I fell stunned.

She picked up the pieces.
One by one she put them together.
Piece by piece she made a whole.

She brought back a man.

XI

Cross-kissed I stagger.

Her face that broke the harbor's beauty
Revokes my passion.

A graciousness redeems.

In the purity of touch,
On the trace of a selfless passion,

Athwart the trajectory of an ancient lust,
I signed a saint.

Her lips, her lips, the mystery of a perfect face!

She bowed her head when Christ broke.
As I wept she smiled.

In the innocence of little children
Her wisdom wells:

My choked desire.

XII

O Christ & Lady
Save me from my law!

O Christ & Lady
Save me from my seed!

O Christ & Lady
Save me from my tongue!

O Christ & Lady
Save me from my curse!

O Christ & Lady
Save me from my moan!

O Christ & Lady
O Christ & Lady

Save me from myself!

XIII

Let no woe be spoken.

Wake not a word.
No haplessness unearth
From any deepness broken.

A timelessness of pain,
An endlessness of love,
The mystery of person.

Redeemed, restored,
She verifies my token:

God is not gone.
Christ is not cold.
The Wound will not worsen.

The Canticle of the Rose

Because in the deepnesses of night you smoulder as a ray that does not
    violate the dark but solemnly defines it;
Because in the resonance of noon you lease a memory of night that
    never blemishes the day but gratefully relieves it;
Because in the hesitance of dusk you mirror gloams that do not shiver
    light from dark but imperceptibly compose them;
I confess thee, and acknowledge thee: in thy mystery of depth I see in
    all thou art the lambent modes of the divine.

Because in the aftermath of time your being does not crumble with the
    past but brilliantly conserves it;
Because in the shaping of the future your spirit does not choke
    eventuality but vibrantly extends it;
Because in the instantaneity of the present your existence does not
    close reality but irrepressibly expands it;
I confess thee, and acknowledge thee: in thy mystery of depth I hear in
    all thou art the voiceless harmonies of God.

For what blooms behind your lips moves ever within my sight the kept
    diffusion of the smile;
And what dawns behind your brow subsists within my thought the
    somnolent mystery of mind;
And what trembles in your words lives on forever in my heart the
    immutable innerness of speech;
Therefore do I confess thee, and acknowledge thee: in thy mystery of
    depth I touch in all thou art the shut profundity of God.

And hear always at night in rivers of sleep the pulsant murmuration of
your voice;
Nor do any words you have uttered but pool in my mind, crisping on
somehow toward my heart's repository cleft,
Potent with implication, unsearchable with wisdom, the haunting and
superlative inflection
Of one who holds the token of her own exemplar, possessing that
preeminence of self, its unselfconscious deftness of response,
Sustaining prescience, an unsurpassable élan of quest, an incontestable
justness of perception.

And have cried out in your arms across my lips those words your
wisdom bore within my sanguinary pain,
And cradled in my heart that nakedness of soul the unblemished
marvel of your flesh made manifest from wisdom's womb,
And traced along those lips the delineaments of a primordial
understanding, modulant of time, the strictures of an irrepressible
blitheness,
And source of that awareness kept without diminution in every tilt and
nuance of your unitary being.

Do not believe because I am man and friable love has addled my brain
so that I speak from daftness only,
Nor ever suppose enchantment feeds exaggeration hoping an induced
reward might grace my love-starved throat,
Nor discount as the elaborate rhetoric of the poet's practional art an
indulgent richness of the luxuriant tongue:
I know too well the accents of excess to be deceived by them,
As he who fashions speech knows better by far its procreant liabilities
than any who listen merely.

(Is it not plain I pile language up to check and impede the rising tide
within me,
Containing in its plex the mastering flood, conserving the vowel-weft
over against its consonantal check,
To hold the importunate crest of my elation, that I might touch the
hidden nerve springing volition free,
And of its concentrated force perfectly specify the fierce insurgent
reck, the absolute object of my attestation?)

But rather, disposed in whatsoever strategem of bland containment
instinct might contrive
My art can err only in insufficiency, my fierce excesses crack on the
ineluctable reality of what you are,
Proving, as a demonstration ever must prove, the meaning not of your,
but my, deficiency,
That anything I utter must emerge but as the pale reflection of your
crucial salient truth,
As words forever are mocked by the essential presences of living fact
preceding them in being.

Therefore do I speak. I cry out. I rejoice. I exult in the uncontainable
triumph of God,
Praising Him in you Who has created you in such profound
extremeness of effectuated being,
And stroked in gratitude kneel in the generosity of that solar Christ
Who blazed you across my life, searing me with your essence;
And I stagger in the excess of that Spirit Who brimmed you with His
fierce charisma,
Expanding utterly beyond your shadowed definition the presage of His
overmastering fact.

And celebrate the truth, knowing that in the cloudy exigence of act
    even the hurtful fission of your faults,
Grievous in time, concatenations of the ancient karmic law inherent
    from Adam,
Eruptive violations darkling with oblique refraction the bond of
    being—
Even the fierce incision of your sins dilate by virtue of your inner
    excellence,
Until the humanity possessed, the received delimitation from which all
    imperfection breeds, subsumes in your clear certitude of choice,
And in the tension trued what you became lifts to an ever greater
    salience of stature.
Caught on your term of truth the human good and the human bad fuse
    on the instant of an unequivocal assent,
And in that attestation you perfectly exist; in that essentiality you *are*.

Just as the general deficiency is healed only in the individual instance,
So I have seen humanity itself enlarged and amplified in your
    preeminence,
Seen sin confirm you, unable to neutralize the latent and subsistent
    truth that is your virtue,
But through a grace endowed become, clenched at your heart, the very
    nexus of perfection,
Throwing into struck relief the magnitude, the matchless capacity of
    unqualified assent,
Determining your arc and high trajectory to complicate, and hence
    enrich, the modulated wonder of your worth.

And hence complete you—one and by one, as you stand free, the
    function of your faults forces the surging shape of your perfection.

You tread them down like shards beneath your feet, or mount upon
them like tall steps to the divine,
Or laugh across them, seeing their useful uselessness in the august
majesty of Christ,
Who came in their delinquence, their work of emptiness, to forge them
in the long majestic function,
And hang them gleaming on the breast of God, deft talismen, the
singular medals of divine reprieve.

Brooked of that unrestrainable volition of response clearly they are
transformed upon the crest of your determination,
And are exalted, as saints' sins only serve to seal their sheer intrinsic
locus of perfection,
Annul themselves against the telling truth by which your virtue lives
transcendent,
Which makes you free, true to that searing shaping work within the
awesomeness that is your soul.

For your sins are generic, the inherited liabilities of time and your
place, the race's tortured trek through all eternity,
Bearing forward in its toil the repressed imbalance of attraction and
repulsion,
Crackling with compressed reaction, its multiple encounters with the
real,
Erupting the pent-up energies of individual volition, as the friable
element, the fractured human soul,
Gropes forward toward its synthesis, the ever-changing shape of
freedom and determination.

But your virtue is specific: in you alone I see those excellencies center
 on the nodal zone of truth,
Personalized within the concrete dimension of gratuitous assent,
Individualized in the subsumed instant of precise volitional judgment,
Perfectly attuned to that comprehensive vision, that unfailing
 suppositum of taste,
And synthesized in the marvelous reflex of a sheer and unpremeditated
 intuition.

For virtue in man is sourced not first in the demarcated, objectivized
 act, the categorical preciseness of a factual achievement,
But rather in that naked rapacity in which the truth perceived is
 grasped and registered,
The irrepressible élan of appetitive gusto, impelling the spirit on its
 sheer incisive quest,
Attesting, by its instantaneous thrust, the flashed preponderance of
 incipient being,
Which it so serves, so follows out, with an intense propensity, the
 ravenous line of its just-glimpsed beatitude,
Constituent of the mystery of the Charity in which vitality and virtue
 both are formed,
And out of which, wild with imminence, God does Himself achieve the
 unmeasured marvel of His scopelessness.

And thus it is precisely in that high clear seizure of the instantaneous
 Truth in which your sanctity is founded,
The fearlessness to seize in faith the brilliant instance of conceived
 perception,
The disposition of that true interior alertness which never brooks the
 imperfections hurting it,

But rather, acknowledging the God of All as Lord and Master,
existential Truth,
Manifests perfections and imperfections each alike as they emerge, the
bright responses of a consummate assent.

Knowing that what is hidden will surely be seen, thrown clear in the
wide eye of day,
Knowing that the sins of the soul are no less there for never having
been committed,
You hold rather to that Lord's decisive provenance of incipient event to
prove the transformation, trusting Him wholly,
Than in the ego's hedging censures and prolaxed equivocal evasions.

For if "all the way to heaven is heaven," then all the way to sainthood is
sanctity,
Painfully teaching that the pure perfection, the luminous chasteness
a holy soul desires,
Was hardly the inchoate state we somehow feel began it, but is rather
The awesome imminence all thwarted nature desperately hopes for
end—
Achieved, if it is achieved, only upon the specific encounters of our
lives, instant by instant,
The ineluctable God bourning the precise gesture of intenseness, the
anguishing stroke
On which the total self, perfection on imperfection, is most acutely
gauged,
Until the soul, at last exposed, shudders under the terrible knowledge,
the inner-awesome truth,
As God defines it through those fierce contextual acts.

"Except your righteousness clearly exceeds the righteousness of
    scribes and pharisees
Ye shall in no wise enter into the kingdom of heaven."
Obsessed, containing privately my abject attitudes, I seemed for a time
    hardly to err,
And in my faultlessness shamed the shameless, a whited sepulcher,
    a pious fraud.
But the saint is rather that jubilant one who in her absolute
    boundlessness of heart
Responds, contrite and joyous, and in the sheer response, proves
    responsible.
Nor fears to stint the living sum of what she is, prescinding from that
    scrupulous reactive guilt,
Whereas my cult of self entailed only a lofty image, momently
    burnished,
Only a hollow shell, however crisply cut, however finely wrought.

For the saints are the lovers: seeing out of a love's excessiveness sin
    shape its coiling strike,
Yet do they bear, they prosper, vice and its ruling virtue subsuming the
    human province,
Our ancient legacy, Adam and Christ, the cockle and the wheat,
    existent together.
This basic, incontrovertible reality, clinched in the fact, serenely
    discloses, stark beneath the beauty, precisely what is there,
Man's every act, hinged on the fractured disposition, jagged beneath
    the choice:
Saint Peter's folly, cruxed on the fierce determining complex, spawn of
    the grinning archetype feeding denial.

Great because he bested, followed a flinchless faith to the jackal-maw
of fear,
But beaten because he boasted, took to himself the option of decision,
Spat out denial to save the polity of rescue, and saw the yawning sin
suck him down,
The o'er-mastering event, greater than he could know, clipped him,
and the cuckoo cock-crow raveled his riddling nerve—
Yet he stood forth, complexed of the guilt-in-faith, a man, and crushed,
and a saint,
Towering on the excessive pinnacle transparent, illumined in the
instancy of failure, his terrible triumphant heart.

So have I seen you weep and rejoice, in your tall moment of corruptive
truth, and stagger into Christ.

And see that deep in the heart's contrition not only are your sins made
nothing (for this we hold in faith)
But burned through love gain an oblique reprieve bought back with a
special grace,
Changed from the generic emptiness all sin can only be into the
veritable agents of perfection,
Momently enforcing, through Christ's vast web of love, the actual
effects of virtue,
And so redeemed, become the factuals of your greatest good, bright
apertures of awareness,
Leaving you radiant, imponderably more potent than ever you were,
Incalculably more cogent than what you could have been or ever you
groped them through,
Giving them back to God in the weaponry of grace, the *felix culpa* of a
redemptive force etched across your heart in hieroglyphs of flame,

The *necessitum peccatum* Christ ever seeks out and needs, as the
surgeon needs the wound,
To prove God's office of perfection, project His timelessness of truth.

It is in Him you touch completeness, and it is in you my
incompleteness cries its lonely name,
As the imperishable image of Woman measures forever incompleteness
in an unperfected man.
Over against my thwartedness of heart you stand, the epitome of
realization,
The epiphany of that unconditional *fiat* God gave when He gave the
world,
The Cosmic Rose of all reality, and which my slit-eyed self is stunned
to glimpse,
But then expands, seizing out of its naked indigence the spacious
valediction of your presence.

You stand inscripted as that ineluctable Other through which the
unpent God marvels Himself.
No night but broods upon your dawn, no dawn but brooks against your
day,
No day but glitters on your sea, no sea but motions to your moon.
My life is crested to your tide-brunt like a keeling ship; I kedge your
deeps,
And through your island latitudes discern those mysteries the lunar
quest propounds.

But mostly it is as pole-star that your realism centers up my night of
faith.
Something unquenchable, something achieved to maximum
intenseness and purity of repose, burns in your being,

Forcing my vague ambivalence to suck toward truth's center. Fastened
    on your beam of truth
How can I waver or deflect and not deny the deepest instance that you
    promise me I am?

And when you draw me on, although my fears shriek with an
    anguished wail in terror at that path,
As the rust-bitten nail shrieks in its violence of extraction drawn from
    the seasoned wood,
I summon the anguish up into one luminous point of pain, and press on
    through,
Walking protected in the measure of your place in heaven, from which
    your being, even now, anticipated,
Casts forth its fierce sheer light, its coiling, torch-like truth.

Thus when you rise at dawn from that deep couch of peace on which
    your sleep is cast,
Your face reveals a wakefulness that day cannot confer, your glass gives
    back a watchfulness no corporal beauty can define,
Your bath restores a youthfulness no natural ardor can have sourced,
For your uniqueness dwells upon no physicality alone, and your
    benignant spirit
Enlivens a repose no unillumined flesh could actuate.

Your very bones bespeak perfection: the conformation of the living
    face, the sutures of the skull.
Out of such depths the Aztec darkness casts its mystery beneath the
    clear Iberian ivory of your skin,
Endowing there the provocative Mexican movement, the modulent
    moment of mangoes and rum, the lambent flesh of the guave,

And those fierce poinsettias that stab the spirit with their perennial
   witness of the flesh.
Their passion daily proves you, and typifies the flashing surfaces
   beneath which glints
The irreducible essence, the marvelous mystery smouldering
   uncontainably on.

And whatsoever death the great indulgent God for you has framed,
   off there, in time's reprieve,
When HE WHO IS will take unto Himself His whole creation
   prefigured in your person,
Know that your image, at once conceived and explicated in the touch of
   time, never can truly die,
But lives immortal in that free transmuted world where all perfection is
   endowed, personified in you, His true creation,
That the stupefied world might thereby know, and knowing love, the
   instance of His vast concern.

And if I call you great, and if I call you holy, and if I say that even your
   sins enforce the sheer reality of what you are,
Know that I speak because in you I gaze on Him, by you I see Him
   breathe, and in your flesh I clasp Him to my breast.
So saying, let me confess the preeminent masterhood that is creation's
   term,
And in your presence salute the transcendent Presence out of which
   you came.
Born of the Father, like Venus from the sea, you bear the beatific
   Ocean's witness of divine abyss,
To pierce, in time, through to the divine abyss from which you briefly
   dawned.

And at that time, though the world must lose the presence of your
    person, your fact will yet live on,
A thing achieved, hence irreducible, God's guerdon and signet that
    completeness, while His own, is yet endowed,
Because He made you in it, the prism of the greater Truth by which
    you are.
In such presence you persist, as in the lesser essence of this poem the
    movement of your breathfulness lives on,
But only as a gloss on what you are, existent only of my speech.

Pride of the presence, bride of the translucent Night, daughter of dawn
    and the resurgent Day,
Bestow on me once more your smile of essence, conferring in your
    grace my own reality,
Endowing as your perfect otherness my shape of man, that freed from
    my sickliness of soul,
I might, in Christ, achieve all that as man I must. And of such grace
Let me once more clasp in my arms the meaning of your fiery spirit,
    and burn upon my heart your perfect signature.

The Rose of Solitude

Her heart a bruise on the Christ-flesh suffered out of locked agonies of
    rebirth.
Her soul fierced inward upon the extravagant passion of woman cut
    between somber and radiant choices.
Her lips panting the Name of God as she thrusts out the tip of her
    tongue for one more drop of His nerving grace.

Solitary Rose! What wall could entomb her? She is all polish and
    ecstasy.
She is all passion, all fire and devotion. She is all woman, in love of God
    bitten by the rapture of God.
She sounds through my mind thirsting the inconceivable excellence of
    Christ.
I hear her feet like rain-clashes run the flat streets to do His will.

All ache. Her heart the glorified Wound. Her soul curls back on its
    pang as the toes of the Christ clutched back on that Nail.
In the stigmata of His gaze her love coils like the flesh on its iron, the
    love-ache of the opening.
When she utters the Holy Name you could never doubt God died for
    the love of man.

Solitary Rose! Unspeakable primacy! The masked and dangerous glint
    of implication!
The gleam of death in the knives of her desire! The crescendos thirsted
    in the strings of her passion!

I have seen in her eyes destinies expand and race out beyond the
    apogees of perfection!

She catches them all! Birds beak for her! In the click of her teeth she
    bites little pieces!
Dance! Dance! Never stint that torrential heart, girl and mother, holy
    immolation,
Free as none else of the vice of the self: that narrow hoard of
    unbroachable stinkings!
In the lift of her head earth glints and sparkles! The seethe of her voice
    is pure as the ecstasy of fire in ice!

Solitary Rose! The Spanish pride! The Aztec death! The Mexican
    passion! The American hope!
Woman of the Christ-hurt aching in moan! God-thirster! Beautiful
    inviolable well-deep of passion!
In the fiercest extravagant love is the tangible source of all wisdom!
In the sprint of your exquisite flesh is evinced the awesome
    recklessness of God's mercy!

The Vision of Felicity

And the terrible
Pang of the heart unhinged,
Bereft of its sources.

Out of the smashed
Light; out of the hard
Unmalleable, abstract
Ferocity of the streets;

Out of the depraved
Human face, horribly
Emptied of its beatitude—

I behold. I behold.

I behold the vision of felicity
And the insuperable human grace.

As one who after mindless torment
Sees surcease in the smile of gratitude,
The plenitude of peace.

Give me my love!
This cry, this cruciform.

Give me back the beauty!

Give me my ache of love
Out of this emptiness!

From the belled
Hell, from the brass
Inferno:

Give me the center back
Of my soul!

New York City

The Raging of the Rose

And the Rose
Rages. Over the Cross
The thorns of denial
Rebuke the egoism of prepossession.
In the imminence of assent
The bloom of essence, actualized,
Unsheaths the storms of existence. Thus it is
That anguish, self-cancellation
Yields into being
The multifoliate particularities of the whole.

In the presence of person
The Rose, invincible, rages and affirms.
Being and Becoming
Realize the sublime synthesis,
The ecstasy of presence.

Son and Mother,
The self-sacrificing God
Immolated on the Tree.
Christ and the Cross
Incarnating irreducibly
The ecstasy of the Rose.

Bride of the world, a nuptial
Consummated unendingly
On the Sword of Spirit.

Tremulous flesh,
Alive with instinct and potentiality,
Deflowered instant by instant:
Over and over the unslakable scepter
Thirsting through the nightfall of the flesh
Its subsistent good.
Flesh and spirit,
Spirit and flesh,
Transmuted together,
Sealed in Christ,
The indwelling.

        He gazes
Out of the very pores of the skin,
The irreducible
Subjectivity of person
Transcending, exceeding in depth,
The whole world of objects,
The whole world of subjects.

      ♦

Dance! Dance!
Dance on the Cross of God,
The cruciform of the Rose!
Dance out the fierce exultancies.
Dance out the rivering apogee of time and its deceptions.
Dance in the heart's redemptive craze
That seizes the shackles of fallen worlds
And annuls their prison.

In the elemental pound of explicit hope
The world restores.
Under the feet of a thousand triumphs
The Cross renews.

In the life of the Rose, the pulsant
Point of mystical intuition,
God immolates Himself,
Makes Himself new. Form
Constellates Being, as the cone of Creation,
Specified,
Meets the cone of the Uncreated,
Specified.

She exults.

♦

And she keeps, she abides, the long
Ecstasy of affirmation, the dynasty of the Rose,
Its raging invincibility, its articulate
Force, its clear
Ethos of truth. As the sun
Bursting out under cloud, its plunge toward earth,
Burns, the coal of itself
One ruby for sunset,
And the conflagration, the rose refulgence,
Purifies the West.

Spurn, in my mind's
Solitary eye,
Voiceless,

Constellated,
The insuperable body
And the sequent grace,
The poem
Breaks,
And out of these long-locked lips,
Out of this throat,
These ventricles,
Toll the throes of celebration,
The canticle of the Rose!

◆

And I
Am free:
Because the spirit
In me
Cries out to the Christ
In her, and is appeased—
The long
Shout of jubilation,
The sole
Syllable of delight.

In the mutuality of this gaze
His cry of love,
Of anguish,
Out of the travail of sensuality
Glimpsing itself beyond the Beloved,
Crying out through the inarticulate web of the senses
Of what is not sensate, rejoicing
Under its cringe of anguish,

Its moan of bliss.
The unbelievable prolongation of the trill of contingency,
An unimpeachable love: this our gasp of delight,
Christ's oath of truth: God's cry.

♦

And so He listens, He answers Himself.
Across long riverings of time He has come.
He arrives,
He gazes,
The smile of these essences bridging Being,
His own meaning is.

We are the metaphors of His certitude,
His power to perfect.
We are the symbols of His supremacy.
We are the mutually inflected beatitude
That yields Him contingency,
Prompts His strike.
In our single gaze
His glimpse beyond finitude
Opens existence.
Not ego, the finite principle,
But presence, Self, *atman:*
The mode of the infinite.

Two egos,
Selfed in unison, moded on the subsistence of Christ,
His single Isness.
She taught me: how one is free,
Possessing freedom in subsistence,

What freedom is.
I taught her: how the crest of emotion,
That freedom,
Is crowned on the undersurge of intellectual passion,
Which is depth.

She taught me: what deliverance is,
The freedom that is salvation.
In truth, in truth,
That the free
Is freedom as truth
Is being,
The crest of release
That liberates freedom
In the primacy of response,
The *act* of existence.

As act, being: His *esse:* to be.

So she: I.
In us: He is.
We Three:
Free.

◆

For in her
All the defects of Woman find their apogee of relevance
And are transfigured: jealousy, suddenness, curiosity,
Vainness, pique, tears, dissimulation, folly—
Ingredients of the essential mystery
Femininity is. Her utterness

Canonizes them each through her sheer
Assertion of being,
Constituents of the feminine mode
That seek their power of reflection,
Ornaments of spontaneity
The scandal of masculine gravity
Established on the due subordination of woman
And the rejection of spontaneity of love.
These she defies,
Not by insolence, as the adventuress
Controverts the stunned world of man
And appropriates its fixtures,
But in the primacy of response,
Essential to the whole of feminine nature
And indigenous to its truth.
Presenting each
To the face of God
She dances,
As the irrepressible daughter
Dances in the doting father's eye,
Supremely confident,
Roguishly certain of what delights him,
Because she knows she typifies
What fatherhood never can be,
And so adores.

◆

You emerge,
Unwombed of the world.
Elemental as the elemental earth,
As lava under the shelves,

As the river in the gorge.
Fierce as the sun, fierce as the high-falling light.
Sudden as waterfalls poured over ledges.
Uncontainable as the swirling torrents of air that plow the globe.
Awesome as the immeasurable storms bourning in from far shores.
Ineluctable as the sea, as restless and as eternal.
Beautiful as being because you possess being.
Elusive as the bird escaped from the fowler.
Wise as the Church because you possess the Church,
For in you, She is.
In you
She achieves Her presence,
Presages Her future.

For out of your womb
Children have come
As souls come forth from the font of baptism.
Out of your heart
Love has come
As Christ came forth from the womb of His mother.
Out of your mind
Wisdom has come
As Idea comes forth from the mind of God.
Out of your lips
Truth has come
As Bread comes forth from the hands of Christ.

Rose! O rareness of the revealed!

Dance! Dance out the truth of being, as act and existence!
Dance up the lineal measurement of time to its quintessence!

Beat it up into synthesis!
Under the storm of your heels
Pound to perfection!
Make it be!
Establish it in your movement,
The perdurable moment that cannot die!
Incarnate it!
Divinize it in your fierce unquenchable essence!
Confer beatitude upon it!
Immortalize it in your glance,
Your look and your laughter!
By the kiss of your lips,
By the ecstasy of your breath,
Re-create it anew!

O clear expression of beauty!
O melody of existence!

Rose!
Reality unfolded!

On the four wings of the Cross,
In the ecstasy of crucifixion,
In the blood of being,
In the single burn of beauty

BE!

So that
In you,

The consummate
Vision of Other:

In you
I AM!

The Integral Years

Tendril in the Mesh

to Susanna

So the sea stands up to the shore, banging his chains,
Like a criminal beating his head on the slats of his cage,
Morosely shucking the onerous staves of his rage. And his custom
Of eyeing his plight, with malevolent fondness, never is done.
For he waits out the span of his sentence, but is undismayed;
He stands and expects, he attends
The rising up, the crest, the eventual slump of the sun.

For he bears in his groin his most precious jewel, the sacred fire of his
    crime,
Who pursued, like the beam of a laser, its solemn command,
Across the shires, red charts of his soul, the wrinkled map of his hand.
    And his heart,
Ridiculous, by someone denied, of a country preferment, never quits,
But clutches its need, like a duck. Somewhere his stain
Discolors the bride of defilement, whom rapine requested, under the
    form of his need, a ventral
Oath. But parched without peace, a swollen defeat, the cunning sleep
    of the slain.

Pluto, regnant occultist, lord of the lorns of lost space, the serene
    distances fringing the skirts of the night,

173

Gleaming back from his visor the farthest, most tentative beam of the
 light,
Whom Kore constrained, with her hesitant breast, above his drooping
 narcissist plant,
To twine in her arms his loud male thong, his truncheon desire, and the
 flex and thrill of his chant.

She was bud. Daughter of Zeus, the Father, whose need Pluto was,
Of the incestuous darkness the daughter provokes in the sire,
When she comes out of the blood; when a menstrual spurt, astart,
 pulses out of her loin,
And she quivers her sleeks, and exclaims, and her mother
Nods and denies, and watches her wander, bait for the god,
Believing it well; though she frowns, she smiles and sighs.

So pitiful Pluto, occultist betrayed, by the quince
Of a maid ensorcelled, daughter of a god, of himself unable,
 succumbed and was drawn,
From the cool of monastic deeps, the slats of his cage, where he beat his
 brains,
Where he knelt in prayer, and shook the chains of his vows,
And clawed his breast in a rage. Persephone smiles,
The pomegranate seed in her pouch, her jewel of rape, and the stain
Of his lust on her lip. She measures his term. Cringing,
He sleeps on unappeased, in the hush of the solemnly slain.

Now sigh the plight of all sires, who groan in their sleep,
When their daughter, divested, glides by in a dream,
Alight with a mauve desire, as of spring,
When barley is born to the year. O sing

174

Of all sires, whose passion, Plutonic, gnarls in the heart
In the immemorial fashion
Of fathers, and groan of the unspeakable thing.

But fight through to the forcing. And, gasping, pull back to see
In the dream if the hymen is crisped on the violent cod like a ring
Of her lips, torn flower, salt clung
Spoil of her triumph. But the aghast heart
Foretells in terror the shrink, the shy inexorable cower
Of the repulsed flesh. But an increase of need.
Oh my God the terrible torch of her power!

I

And it creams: from under her elbow a suffix of light, a sheen of kept
    being,
What the gleam from along her arm prefigures of quest.
I sense over slopes a rondure of presence invoked.
In the small of the girl, where hips greet the waist,
A redolence lurks in the crease, a rift of repose.

And I take in a long loop of arm everything seascapes prefigure of
    dusk:
Sycamore-sweeps, the tableaux of massed chaparral, a rouse of rowans.
Let sea-licked winds wrap the inch of their roots with evening
There to compose what the chewn leaves of the tan oak pucker up on
    the tongue;
And there, like a wand, wonderment's long awakening, strong
    shaftings of light.

No, never. Not one shall survive. When two such as we are
     outlaunched on desire, neither one comes back.
We have staked out our bodies on mesas of glimmering vetch.
We have mapped territorial claims on plateaus ripe for inclusion.
Sentinels spring up alarmed: the guardians of places remote are alerted
     to cover our foray.

Scalptakers, yes. And have waited out eons of stealth to stalk our
     quarry.
Now our needs converge; we join in a scuffle of perns.
The nets and the spears of beaters off there in the dark enflank us.
When the cry of the hunter broke over the flesh we fled them afar.
We emmeshed our bodies in thickets, entoiled in the brush.

I am old as the prairies and wise as the seams of worn granite, but she is
     new burgeoned.
New as the minted tin, as sleek as the calmness of ivory engravers have
     tooled for emblems.
A girl like the glide of an eel, like the flex of a serpent startled.
But I catch her in throes of pulsation; we are wantoned in groves.

Crotch and thigh; she is reft. Let me break white flesh asunder to cock
     this woman.
In the glimmer of night a wedge of fern configures her croft.
Maidenhair snuggles the cleft. Its shadow conceals and defines.
When I dip my lips to drink of that spring I throat the torrent of life.

For passion subsumes: what is focused is fixed, denotes its spang of
 vector.
A long supple swell of belly prescinds from extinction.
When I reach above for the breasts my arm is a laser unleashed.
I have knifed through dooms that spelt long since the death of man's
 spirit.

I have fastened my heart on the stitch of your voice, little wince of
 delight in the thicket,
Where the slim trout flick like a glint of tin in the pesky shallows.
Salacity keels; our itch of an ardent desire consumes and engorges my
 being.
I cannot look on your face; but my fingers start toward pockets of peace
 that lurk in your armpits.

Wild stallions of shuddering need squeal jumps of joy at your whistle.
I feel them snort in my ribs, they snuff for foods long bilked in their
 pleas for existence.
Now they snook and are all transfigured in sudden aerial manoeuvres.
They skip like gnats in the shafts, made mad of your moan.

Give me your nipples to lip and your ribs to caress,
Take down from your shoulders the silks that have baffled the sun.
But retain as your own the cordage of menacing loves,
Those fingers of others before me that seethed and passioned,
Those hungers you held in the crimp of your flesh, confounding
 possession.

For I sense the pungence of death alert in your loins, little woman:
All men in the past who have lain on the wand of your body.
Your belly is seeded with sperm, the slick of lovers cinctures your waist
   like the wake of snails.
I cannot expunge from your flesh what they wrought, or annul their
   passion.

But do not withhold from my gaze what from everyone else you
   concealed:
The remotest part of your heart that you kept immured like a jewel.
When I touch it to see in your eyes the sheerest expansion of terror,
To taste on your stretched out tongue as you die the tensile nerve of its
   anguish,
I know I have fastened the nail, I have quicked your core of existence.

For I am the actual. Telluric forces are groined in my being.
Uranian urgencies coil of their strengths in my soul's narrow passes.
Out of my sinews deep starts of hunger yield mixed epiphanies:
The snake that sleeps in the stones and comes forth out of winter;
The great cat of the mountain that stalks for fawns in the darkening
   barrows.

I am the grizzly that grapples his mate in his hug of sheerest survival,
The salmon that jells his milt on the clutch his woman has sown in the
   gravel.
I am the river that breaks its back and pitches into the bay,
The osprey that jackknifes sidewise in surf to talon his quarry.

And I am the sea, its music, its instinct and whisper.
I encurl your rocks with my spill and embrace your shoulders.
In my estuary arms I entwine and enfold your thighs, I sleek your
buttocks.
On my girth you toss like a chip to the crest of crude torrents.
When the great ships put out of port across my presence
Their seahorns chant me, sing mournful tones of presaging loss.

No ridge but the bone crest of power in the continent's nape.
A glaze of light is riddling the sheen of the wheat of Tehema.
Have the winds of Point Reyes, festooned with spindrift, declared
anything other?
Do they glare for the spoil of the sun? Do they ache for the couches of
night?

No bridge avails but the stretched out flesh of its coupling hunger.
Between the split of your thighs I plant spurts of voracious pleasure.
Not a hair of the nock that a woman widens anent the cob resists of a
love.
On the nodes of transparent worlds we collapse, we pant and expire.

In all darks is my joy defined, that plaza, those nubian porches,
There my whole tongue turns in the col of your beating body.
In my hands of a man the sense is awake to mold idols of flesh for
victims.
Plunged to the wrists I feel passion spurt through the instincts meshed
in your nerves,
The peaks of clitoral quickness jetting spunk in a viscid issue.

You come back to be coaxed: I have caught you between the cheeks
    and will never be stinted.
Entwined in your thirst I tangle hair, the riatas of your desire.
In order to crest I snake angles of coupled completeness.
A flinch of fire, something struck from the meshes of passion, clusters
    my neck.

Do not think to be stronger than death; to die is to drink desire.
To die is to take at the pitch of madness one fabled stroke of disinterest.
I have felt on those fields the light that a passion decreed, spined on
    sheer splendor.
When you moan and expire shrewd arrows of truth, shot through
    shields of zinc, pierce my belly.

Now I ken where suns have gone down when they quitted our country.
It is not as if they had nothing to gain in defaulting.
Rather with us for cause they seek stratas, new zones of extinction.
They annihilate zeros, total steeps to expunge; like us, they erase their
    condition.

Now my fingers conclude. They have founded whole sweeps of
    existence,
Have soaked up splendor in jets, have fed to the final.
No trace remains of what was; across the line of my life
Your breast pounds and proves; the sound of your heart extols its
    ancient surrender.

II

Man of God. Tall man, man of oath. Mad man of ignorant causes.
Like the mast of a ship, like the weathered spar of a schooner.
Long shank of a man, whose hair is all whetted with frost, and a nick of
    silver.
What inch of enactment cinctured your loins and is freed?
I can feel in my knees the scruff of time's thrust as you take me.

Finger of God! A stipple of terror shudders my skin when you touch
    me!
Who are you? In your eyes is the passion of John the Baptist and the
    folly of Christ!
Do not drop me! I have never been known of man, really, before you
    possessed me!
By all men, of any, who have bruised and straightened my body,
The marks of their hands are erased of your lips. I never knew them!

Now teach me your deeps! Prophet and utterer of godly imponderable
    oaths, great prayers of anguish.
Guru of my bed, who have taught me koans of revealment.
Adept of niches and slots, my woman's being convulses in truth for
    your entry!
When your hands work marvels I fear I will die, will faint in your
    swells of compression.

Let rivers that run to the sea be my attestation.
You took me on Tamalpais, in the leaf, under Steep Ravine redwoods.
The bark of trees was broken to tear and divest me.
On the brow of the hill that brinks its base you thrusted me up to your
    God.

Beast and Christian! What manner of dog do you worship for Christ
    that you must rend and devour!
I have felt in my womb the index of Him you call God.
Do you wasten life that my flesh and my bone should be wholly
    consumed of your spirit?
What is His face if the eyes you blaze are the tusks of carnivores?

I have no defenses against your truth and desire none.
Make me a Christian, then do what you want with this dross,
For a strange pale fury that cannot be natural consumes me.
I blink back tears of relief to feel in your hands the awe of Him you
    adore.
Is your vow of a monk meant to serve for the seal of your lust?

For your lust of a monk is a hunger of all God's seekers.
In my nerve's raw marrow I feel Him teach me His witness.
Let me go! But do not desert what you chose to instruct.
If I cannot reckon what unstrings my knees what worth is survival?

Let me go! No, but breach my belly with godly unspeakable anguish!
This split of thighs you desire is more than my means.
Your face is flensed with an awesome devouring passion.
In the flukes of contortion I fear what I see as I need it.
My body is written with poems your fingers enscrolled on my flesh.

Let no woman survive me, old man, mad man of the mountain,
Wily old buck of the benches and bull elk of somnolent mesas.
Monk of the seashore and friar of granite enclosures,

The mad holy man who spread my legs for entry.
As the crotch of cloistered enclosures my flesh is empaled on your
    spirit!

III

And the storm swings in from the sea with a smashing of floats.
There are hulks on the rocks where wrecks broke splintering up under
    waves.
A kindling-making wind is tearing out scrub on the jaw of the hill,
And the encompassed bay where fishermen loafed is found a cauldron
    of spume.

Let it blow! Now a wild rejoicing of heart springs up in answer!
After summer's stultification what more can penetrate deadness?
The nerves that have slept for so long in the simmering flesh,
    complacent with languor,
Awaken to swing their stutter of fright at the crash of billows.

And those casual loves are swept out. Only a troth as stark as the tooth,
Elemental and sheer as the hurricane's whetstone incisor;
Only a love as crunched as the jaw of the cougar,
When the passion-responders grope for each other under the pelt of the
    storm.

They will find in the rain what can match the spatter of hail on a house.
They will know where to slake when the trees break free of what heaps
    at their knees.

And they moan. Couched on beach grass under shelter of drift
They hug each other. They watch with the zeal of love the hurricane's
    howl.
With one eye bent to the weather they see the light on the head at Point
    Reyes
Hum like an axhead held to the stone, the sparks a spurt shooting
    leeward.

Now crawl to me shivering with love and dripping with rain,
Crawl into my arms and smother my mouth with wet kisses.
Like a little green frog slit the cleft of your thighs athwart me.
The rain on your face is the seed of the stallion strewn as it spits blue
    fire.

For the lightning forks like one naked the seething thud of the sea.
And swells like a woman's in birth when she heaves up her belly.
She has braced her heels on the land; her beaches are benched to that
    passion,
And her crotch is the hollow, sunk low under wind-heap waves, when
    its back breaks over.

She is fouled of bad weather but never of love, this woman.
In her blood the groan and travail of a birth is being fashioned.
Her spilth like the gasp of stallions clings round her ankles.
And her vulva tilts thwart the wind's wide lip when he whistles his
    force through her body.

Now crawl to me under this driftwood hutch and cower upon me.
Warm the stitch of rain in the drench of passion and forget to be
    frightened.

But build in your womb's young realm the germ of your mother the
   sea.
For to be found in this labor sunk under a shelf she was nothing loath of
   her mating.

Oh splendor of storm and breathing! O woman! O voice of desire!
Tall power of terminal heights where the rain-whitened peaks glisten
   wet!
But the heave of slow-falling sleep will follow outpouring in winter's
   wake.
This too is your meed when passion is flashed for blood in the
   typhoon's crater.

Now sleep in my arms, little newt, little mite of the water,
Little wind-beaten frog, pale delicate limper alone on sea-pulled
   pebbles.
Go to sleep and awaken in spring when your blood requickens.
And bear back to man in your flesh the subtle sign of him who marked
   you for God.

IV

Daughter of earth and child of the wave be appeased,
Who have granted fulfillment and fed the flesh in the spirit.
A murmur of memory, a feint of infrequent espousals,
And the tug of repose the heart hovers and tilts toward dawn.

Somewhere your body relinquishes creeds of defiance.
I have tasted salt salience, and savored its fragrance, have crested
   repose.

Now appeasement crouches and wends its way through my being.
I sense fulfillment not breached of strings and torches.

Kore! Daughter of dawn! Persephone! Maiden of twilight!
Sucked down into Pluto's unsearchable night for your husband.
I see you depart, bearing the pomegranate seed in your groin.
In the node of your flesh you drip my flake of bestowal.

What will you do, back on earth, when you find your mother?
Will the trace of dark lips fade out of your flesh forever?
I have knocked your instep with rapture, I have wounded your flank.
Like the little fish in the dredger's boat you bear the teeth of the gaff.

O daughter of God! When the sons of man covet your passion,
Do not forget who placed on your brow his scarab of sovereign
    possession.
In the service of holy desire bear truth for escutcheon.
And when you return to the roost of night wear the mane of the sun!

EPILOGUE

Dark God of Eros, Christ of the buried brood,
Stone-channeled beast of ecstasy and fire,
The angelic wisdom in the serpentine desire,
Fang hidden in the flesh's velvet hood
Riddling with delight its visionary good.

Dark God of Eros, Christ of the inching beam,
Groping toward midnight in a flinch of birth,
The mystic properties of womb and earth:
Conceived in semblance of a fiercer dream,
Scorning the instances of things that merely seem.

Torch of the sensual tinder, cry of mind,
A thirst for surcease and a pang of joy,
The power coiled beneath the spirit's cloy,
A current buckling through the sunken mind,
A dark descent inventive of a god gone blind.

The rash of childhood and the purl of youth
Batten on phantoms that once gulled the soul,
Nor contravened the glibness in the role.
But the goad of God pursues, the relentless tooth
Thrills through the bone the objurgation of its truth.

Often the senses trace that simmering sound,
As one, ear pressed to earth, detects the tone
Midway between a whisper and a moan,
That madness makes when its true mode is found,
And all its incremental chaos runs to ground.

Hoarse in the seam of granite groans the oak,
Cold in the vein of basalt whines the seed,
Indemnify the instinct in the need.
The force that stuttered till the stone awoke
Compounds its fluent power, shudders the sudden stroke.

Dark Eros of the soul, Christ of the startled flesh,
Drill through my veins and strengthen me to feed
On the red rapture of thy tongueless need.
Evince in me the tendril in the mesh,
The faultless nerve that quickens paradise afresh.

Call to me Christ, sound in my twittering blood,
Nor suffer me to scamp what I should know
Of the being's unsubduable will to grow.
Do thou invest the passion in the flood
And keep inviolate what thou created good!

The Narrows of Birth

Christmas night: the solstice storm
Muttering in retreat, threatening rain,
Cypress witlessly clawing the roof,
Its vague hand scrawling the obscure
Prophecy of reprisal. Across the dunes
Wind rakes the hollow-breasted sea,
Coughing and expectorating like a consumptive invalid,
A feverish old woman racked in senility's
Festering decrepitude, morbidly ailing.

I awake from a dream of ritual slaying: beachfire
Back from the surf; hunched in an angle of logs and driftwood
Crouches the clan. Among them,
Free and unsuspecting, a youth lounges,
Perfectly relaxed, a man
Stalwart, high-minded and virile,
In the deceptive way the dream
Inveterately falsifies reality,
Approximating the ideal.
To me, in the freezing awareness of apprehension,
It becomes increasingly apparent
He is not to be their guest but their victim.
Yet my very prescience, which declares my involvement,
Renders me powerless. For I have entered into complicity,
A kind of unspoken pact, with these people, seeking something
They have which I need, which I once knew and lost,

And have come to recover in my own quest;
And because of this need, this involvement,
Have forfeited my freedom.

And suddenly, with great clarity of vision,
I see them for what they are,
The castrate sons and the runt daughters,
Maimed progeny of the Mother,
From whose destiny I myself, long ago, had somehow escaped,
And have returned now, improvidently,
To verify my lack. They hobble about their appointed tasks,
Preparing the terrible rites of immolation.
They seem to be concocting some kind of revolting brew,
The narcotic that renders the victim senseless,
Of which the elements, I am aware, are parlous:
Milk and dung, blood and semen, menses and afterbirth,
The mordant ingredients of parturition.
These, I see, stand for the universal postulates of generation:
Twin compulsions of Desire and Death:
The inexorable forces which every major religion
Has pitted itself to overcome; and from which
The vows of every monk
Are structured toward deliverance.

And I sense, from the depths of this recognition,
The utter ineffectuality of everything I am—my own monk's vows
Jettisoned in a spasm of precipitate repudiation,
Leaving me weaponless, hands utterly empty,
To grope my way back to these somnambulists,
These ominous dark sources,
In the reassessment of my life.

Across the fire I face the matriarch,
My ancient ancestress, the fountainhead of my blood,
Saying, "I have come back, Mother,"
And I bow my head as a penitent
Bows for absolution; or as the prodigal,
Having squandered his heritage,
Lowers his neck to signify his wrong.
But in the old mother of glittering eyes
Is neither absolution nor forgiveness.
Her gaze searches me narrowly,
Unrelenting, utterly unimpressed
By anything I might say,
Waiting for proof. She will be appeased now
Only by deeds—by words
Never.

      I waver in the firelight,
Uncertainly, unable to know
What it is I am to do, unable to reassert
Who I am, or say what brought me here,
What motive or what reasons avail
In this weirdly familiar place.

The plotting goes on.
I see the body of the youth,
Beautifully muscled, like Michelangelo's
Immortal slave, the raised shirt
Banded about the nipples,
And all the magnificent body
Slumped in its unmistakably erotic swoon.

The castration begins.

I wake to the dawn, bolt upright,
With the retreating storm
Muttering in the eaves, uncertain
And vague and foreboding.
I feel beside me in the strange bed
The body of my young wife.
She is breathing deeply in sleep,
The clear pulse of her being
Mustering within it all the life-force
Against my fear. In the next room
Her nine month's son cries out, softly,
Under the wince of my pervasive torment,
An anguish which haunts the house,
My pain and my guilt.
In the stretched silence
I touch her again, the flank of woman,
Modulant with the subsumed
Rapture of life. And everything I have come for
Clutches my throat,
Warring in the narrows of this birth.

The Challenge

Then what do I seek?
Truly, I know not.

           Destiny,
The oblique force of my being,
Evicted me from a measured life,
The austere life of perfection.

It thrusted me
Back into the convulsive and uterine world,
Where the animal cry
Bellows at the gate,
Where the engine and the beast
Groan in travail.

In this my certitude,
My sole conviction
Is that my nature does not lie,
That destiny and nature are one.

Clearly my soul's trial,
Its naked ordeal,
Lies in this acceptance:
The reconciliation of what I believe
With the fact of what I am.

This is the wound that tears me apart.
Neither peace of spirit
Nor serenity of soul,
Till that gap closes.

◆

Why, then, do I fight it?
What is the fester, the seething sore
Refusing to heal?

Pride? That the lofty
Pinnacle of aspiration,
At the eleventh hour of life,
Slipped from my grasp?

Or a morose preoccupation with image,
The disconsolate craving for the high religious profile
The habit of the monk gratuitously confers?

Or mere stubbornness,
A mulish refusal to accept the obvious,
The fact that I failed?

All these and more.
They name the fester;
They do not constitute the wound.

Something seethes beneath them,
More mysterious,
More keen and more blind.

Something lives on that the heart can't help,
Something below the proud flesh of that bruise:
A hunger for God and nothing but God
This world cannot fill.

Neither wife nor child nor fame nor fortune.

The brute thirst for the absolute,
The apotheosis of desire
In the guts of God.

What?
The reconciliation of what I believe
And what I am?

Rather
Desire slaked in its raw Source.
Intelligence stunned in its Prey.

◆

For in the monastery
What I believed and what I am
Truly *were* one—

Up to a point!

But beyond that point
Something rebelled.

(Not in my spirit:
No real reservation
Troubled my spirit.)

But something more visceral.
Something I can only call
The subsistent self,
The basis of my being.

As a monk
I sought to immolate this subsistent self
In the interest of transcendence
And for years it availed.

But after a time
That basic being climbed down from its cross,
Embracing its need,
Thirstily,
And refused to return.

No matter how I implored.
No matter how I threatened and cajoled.
No matter how I appealed to the supreme imperatives,
The fiery strictures—

(No matter! No matter!)

It would not go back.
It refused to return.

But rather, when the woman came,
It followed her out,
Back to the wild convolutions,

The mouthing and the tonguing,
The bitterness and the dross.

Leaving the spirit stunned.
Leaving the mind sick.
Leaving the soul sullen.

Until, realizing at last
Nothing more could change now,
Nothing save itself alone,
The mind gave over.

In the anguished need for unification
The malleable mind
Relinquished and succumbed.

And now *it* endures crucifixion,
It endures torment and incertitude.
For the spirit's belief,
The soul's conviction,
Lie back in the cell.

♦

Somewhere there exists
The crystal prism,
The clear point of reconciliation,
This I know.

To find it is my challenge.

But its shape remains shut,
Closed against the surging myth of futurity,
In the legend of the past—

The dark, blood-ooze origin of things,
The spurt of birth.
And that, after all, is the gasp of completion.

Let then my basic being,
That savageness of soul,
Project the guerdon of its need.

Then my cross-stretched mind
Will grope the deliverance
This flesh could not abide.

The Scout

Passing a leathercraft shop in Mill Valley I see
Yellow buckskin, long undulant fringes,
Lazy-stitch beadwork of the Plains tribes,
Strong, tawny wear of the old frontier.

Buckskin right now is a youthful fad, but not
This grade of the authentic. And turning inside,
On the moment's crystalline decisiveness,
I allow myself to be fitted. The cost:
A hundred dollars down, a hundred
Dollars on delivery. I pay
Without a quiver. Returned home,
I muse by the fire, smoking,
The first of a few slow nights reflection
Before the garb is my own.

For the implications
Are revolutionary. Tonight, back in the monastery,
My black and white habit is worn by another.
But now, in the shimmering imagination,
I assume the regalia of the Old West:
Beads, buckskin and bearclaws, the extravagant
Fantastic image. Yet for all the grandiose
Self-projection, which time must erase to confirm,
I know I have come to a steep divide,
A fork in the crooked trail of my life;

That I have truly chosen; will bear that choice;
Wear it about my being, as I learned to bear it,
As I learned to wear it over long years,
In the habit of the monk.

                    For a way opens up
Taking me instinctively back,
Back beyond the first frontier, beyond the advent
Of agriculture or the civilized dream,
Back to the Stone Age myth and the ethos of blood.
These rare integuments are its powerful insignia,
A way of ordering what, to the imagination,
Is truly there but rationally denied, and hence
Vague, without substance, lacking essential symbolic force—
Back beyond the confirming vineyard of my youth,
That took me out of my father's world, setting me free—
Back to the archaic mysteries,
The fertility of the soil, the magic of animals,
The power-vision in solitude, the terrifying
Initiation and rebirth, the love
And ecstasy of the dance, modalities
Governing the deeps of instinct,
The seat of consciousness itself,
Where the poet, as shaman to his time,
Ritualizes for the race—all, all subsumed
In the skin of the bison and the antler of the elk,
And borne on the being. Just so
The habit of the monk, received in solemn investiture,
Confirms its tangible ethos, feeds
Participation to the flesh, yields
The meaning it denotes.

Or so in my musing.
But suddenly a mounted figure rises in my mind,
Abruptly accosting. The single
Eagle feather of the scout marks him Protector,
Watcher of the Spirit, Guardian of the Sacred Mysteries,
Keeper of the Pass.

I raise my hand,
Palm forward, the immemorial gesture of peace.
But wheeling his pony he disappears.
I am left apprehensive, touched by a strange foreboding,
Vaguely disturbed.

Gazing into the flame-lick
I catch for the first time the vibration of menace.
I smell danger at the divide.

The Black Hills

Riding a horse up a narrow gorge I pick
Traces of an old trail. In my dream
All is weed-grown, brush-choked, my clothes
Tear on quick spines, and here and there
Thorns have scratched blood. Suddenly in the abrupt dusk
My horse spooks and whinnies, refusing to go on.
I dismount and drag forward, exasperated, the bridle
Straining in my left fist as I shoulder through,
Press on and in to a lost clearing.
Then I see, obliquely up-slope, skewed in stark branches,
The ancient tree-burials of the Indians.
This is the place. I have reached at last
My dark quest's end.

        For it was here,
At the close of the final bloodily-doomed campaign,
A band of exhausted Sioux, burying their dead,
Endured ambush. United States cavalry,
Charging down-slope at dawn, leveled
The ritual-keeping remnant. Braves, squaws,
Even the cradleboard papoose—all alike
Riddled under the skirl of lead
From the snout carbines. Scalped, mutilated,
The sex of the women hacked out with bowie knifes,
Jabbed over saddlehorns, to be worn
Swaggering back to the stockade saloons,

Derisive pubic scalps, obscene trophies
Of a decimated people, a scalped land.

Left here the bodies
Made whitened skeletons under the tree-hung graves.
Then blizzard and grizzly scattered about the little clearing
The buzzard-picked bones. With the next spring thaw
Dispersed remnants of other bands found their way here,
Collected the littered remains, grouping them into awkward bundles,
Pathetic attempts to reshape the dead,
And hoisted them skyward, joining the earlier
High tree-burials the Plains Indians use on the vast prairies
When the earth is frozen, and now, strange transplants,
Adapted here in the shortness of time
To the dark mountains, the dense firs.

The dust of battle is all washed away with the years.
But the sky-hung mummies still survive the snows.
I see their tattered shrouds
Flutter in the night-wakened wind
That prowls down the canyon.

But my terrified horse balks unmanageably.
Contorted at the clearing's edge he plunges and shrieks.
Thinking it no more than the spectral graves
Terrorizing the acute nostrils and the fearful animal sight,
I tether him short and grope forward alone.
But suddenly the intangible presence tormenting him
Transfixes me. Nailed to the spot

Terror like an electric vibration rivets my being.
Confused, immobilized, fighting to retain consciousness,
I sense the ominous locus, the magnetic spot
From which all that threatens
Issues toward me.

It pours from a spill of shattered boulders
Just beneath the sky-swung graves.
Here the last braves took refuge,
Fought till every arrow was gone,
Fought till the white man's
Pitifully malappropriate firearms
Fell silent in their hands,
Fought with knifes arced and the tomahawks
Screaming like insane eagles,
Hacking and whirling over the melee
When the cavalrymen charged in,
Blasting, kicking, gouging,
The pistols spitting till the last riddled body
Jerked limp and flopped dead.

Gazing toward the cluster of rocks
I gather into focus the incredible emanation,
The torrent of hatred pouring into me.
It is as archaic and irreducible as weightless stone,
A kind of psychic lava,
Pouring across the narrow space
And the cavity of the years.

And it is male.
The savage violence.
The primal pride.

For this have I come.

And seeking to master it, to neutralize
The hate, convert
Power to purpose in the need that brought me here,
I project in my imagination the sublime
Patriarchal image I reverenced as a boy,
The composite visage of all the great chiefs,
Their names and singularities: Roman Nose, Black Kettle,
Red Cloud, Crazy Horse, Gall, Sitting Bull . . .
Confronting the torrent of malediction
I wring that image from my buried past,
And give it life.

But the vision fades.
The white man's guilt, founded in my heart,
Warps between, a massive, misshapen block.
I see only the piebald ponies,
Retreating, their tails
Flattened before the blizzard of time,
Humpbacked under the weight of the years,
A splendor despoiled, a ravished pride.

"Father," I cry, "Come back to us!
Return to our lives!"
My words ring through the dusk,
And a wind springs up, rattling the leaves.

"I have come to close the wound,
Heal the gash that cuts us from you,
And hence from the earth!"
I pause, listening intently,
Aware of the unanswering gloom, the dusk
Muffled and intense.
"I have come to bury the hatchet,
That we who must live
May live in peace!"

Something moves there in response,
Of this I feel sure,
But no light remains to let it be seen.
Only, from the heap of rocks,
Like an answering hail of arrows,
The torrent of hate.

I sink to my knees shouting:
"Give me your blessing!"
There is rain in the air now
And no time to lose.
I expose my lacerated hands,
The ancient sign that suffering proves one true.
Leaning into the blast of repudiation
I sway desperately, a lost scout
Swaying on the frozen prairie,
In the killing cold.

Aware only of the unrelenting force
Pouring over and around and through me
I lift my head as the night closes down

And shout the one thing left,
The old, hopeless human attestation:
"I love you!"

The force of malediction
Increases to something almost physical.
And indeed the actual wind,
Pouring down the canyon,
Rises to a roar, bearing a volley of torn leaves,
Twigs, loose bark, flung gravel.

And suddenly the rain begins.

Crouched in the weeds
I summon up again the vision of the chiefs,
Call them back in consciousness:
The painted shields and the war ponies,
The painted bodies and eyes,
Buffalo hats, the lynx-skin headdresses,
An eagle feather dangling for every slain foe;
Rippling war-bonnets trailing to the heels,
The jewel-work of beads and the delicate
Fancy-stitch of porcupine quills, arrow quivers
Furred with the magic skin of the otter—
For an instant I possess it again,
The fabulous, unspeakable vision,
Primitive and elegant,
The unquenchable glory of primal man.

Then it fades. A sudden
Spasm of hysteria doubles me up.

I relapse into uncontrollable sobbing.
"I love you," I scream. "Can't you hear me?
God damn it, I love you!"

◆

I wake up shouting. I am in my own bed,
Rigid beside my young wife.
It is hours before dawn.
I rise wordlessly, without making a light.
Shaken and trembling, I grope my way to the adjoining room.
On the grate a few coals
Gleam in the fireplace,
Remnants of last evening's blaze,
Dying in ash. A flood of moonlight
Pours through the window. Standing naked in the dark
I let the feeble warmth of the embers
Caress my cold shins.
I gaze shudderingly into the darkness,
Still plunged in the awful atmospherics of the dream.
Moonlight glows on an improvised mandala
I have fashioned out of my mute desire
And hung in the room:
Two gigantic eagle claws
Fixed above the black and white
Pony-tail braid-ends of the Flathead tribe,
Pinned on a Navajo saddle blanket
And nailed to the wall.
The claws clutch upward. I placed them so,
Following the ghostly eagle's death-flight,
Which left life behind and flew at the sun, its father,
Flew till the great unreal talons

Took peace for prey,
Exultantly, their death beyond death,
Stooped upward, and struck
Peace like a white fawn
In a dell of fire.

I believe it. And believing as well
That what we wear and how we wear it
Bodies forth our hope, the deep implication of our underlying need,
I turn to the adjacent wall where, flanking the eagle-claw mandala,
My great buckskin coat hangs in the moonlight.
I have placed it high on the wall,
As my religious habit, hung high on the door of the monastic cell,
Stood sentinel there
Against the intrusion of the world.
New and untried, like a novice's tunic,
The close-fringed coat yet typifies a faith, the image
Of all I seek to recover in my urgency of quest.

But now, in the aftermath of the dream,
The bravery of buckskin jeers me derisively.
Even as I gaze the Navajo saddle blanket
Glows with the pallor of death,
Some tattered burial wrapping
Salvaged from my dream.

Out on the dunes
The sea falls conclusively,
A muffled, explosive gasp,
Final as doom.

But opening the door
The drench of moonlight embraces me,
A sudden inundation of suffused radiance.
It is the beautiful, unsullied present,
Eternally renewed, eternally reborn.
And it envelops me, and blesses me.
I look up into its immensity and its love,
Its past-dispelling love.
And standing there in the doorway,
All Indian at last,
I lift up my arms and pray.

♦

But it is too much—
Too heartbreakingly much.
Shivering I turn back to bed.
The ghost of what was,
All that never again can be,
Bodiless and fleshless,
Gleams in the eagle claws,
A spectral presence as I pass by.

Suddenly I jump like a man stabbed.
Under my feet something cracks sickeningly and collapses.
It is only a plastic toy,
The dropped plaything of my wife's infant child.
But reaching down I feel blood on my thumb,
Where the bones of all the buffalo
Gashed my heel.

Dark Waters

Chipmunk: slash with quick teeth
These rawhide ropes.

Little fox, sleek cat of the thicket,
Puma, ringtail in the quaking bush,
Mink in the meadow.

Weasel-woman:
Drive devils out of my blood.
Scare off fear.

I have made a long run.
I have swum dark waters.

I have followed you through hanging traps.
I have risked it all.

O cut my thongs!

At the fork of your flesh
Our two trails come together.

At your body's bench
I take meat.

Storm-Surge

Christmas Eve, night of nights, and Big Creek
Is on the move. At the equinox
Tempting rains toyed with us, teasing, and offshore at sea,
Beyond the slant sandbar blocking the rivermouth,
The great grey salmon skulked in the trough, dreaming the long
Genetic dream, plasmatic slumber of the unfulfilled,
Awaiting the moment of the forth-showing,
The river-tongue in the sea's vulva,
The strength in the slot.

First incremental showers
Flushed dead vegetation, cathartic,
Purging the veins of the cleft mountain.
Then a month of drought reimposed itself,
The turbid summer's condign sterility
Drying the glades, sucking the flow back into the hills,
As if the mountain begrudged what it gave, called back its gifts,
Summoning them home, the high largess
Repentant of its grace.

Advent broke dry,
December harsh on the hills, no sign of cloud
On the steely horizon. But solstice
Brought respite: a northwest flurry
Shook the last limbs bare, the drum of hailstones
Rattling the shingles under riddled cloud.
Then wind swung south and the nimbus struck,

One thousand-mile storm enveloping the coast,
Forty-eight hours of vertical rain, water falling
Like the splurge of God, the squandering of heaven—
As if forever on the mountains and the draws,
As if forever on the river-forks and creeks,
As if forever on the vast watershed, its sheer
Declivities, its seaward-pitching slides,
Thirst-shrunken slopes of the parched ridges.

And I lean in the dark, the harsh
Pulsation of night, Big Creek
Gorged in torrent, hearing its logs
Hit those boulders, chute that flood,
Batter their weight to the sandbar
And the sea, ripping a channel
Out to the future, the space beyond time,
On the eve of the coming, when Christ,
The principle in the purpose,
Splits the womb in his shudder of birth.

Steelhead

Incipient summer, scorch of the sun,
And the great steelhead shows up in our creek.
He lies in a pool, the shallow basin of a thin rock weir,
Impassively waiting. Ten days go by
And still he lingers. His presence
Is inscrutable. No one around here
Recalls such a thing: steelhead
Landlocked in summer.

                     For the tag-end of April
Sees the last of them. Unlike all salmon,
Rising in winter to die at the spawn,
Steelhead commonly wrig back to sea,
Reclimbing the river-path year after year:
Continuous the trek, the journey joined;
Indomitable the will, the life-thrust.

But this? this aberration?
What is its meaning, and why here?
Deeper hideouts, below and above,
Where salmon and steelhead alike at the spawn
Await their time—those same deep holes
Are perfect places to bide out the drought
Were such his purpose. But no. Dangerously exposed,
In window-pane water he lies alone,
And waits. Inexplicably waits.

Dreaming last night I stiffly arose,
Groped my way down through scarred slopes
To a shallow pool. I knew it for his.
The moon, gibbous, lacked light to see by,
But sensing him there I made vaguely out,
Alone on the bottom like a sunken stick—
No, like a God-stoned monk prostrate in his cell—
That enigmatic shape, sleeplessly intent.
Daunted, I left him alone in that hapless place
And crept back to bed.

     To go down in the dawn,
Seeking him out as in my dream,
Holding him there in my mind's eye,
Still pointed upstream, smelling the high
Headwaters, while all about him
The dance of life sweeps rapturously on—

Giddy with delight the moths fly double.
In a spasm of joy the mayflies breed.
Above on the bank our Labrador bitch,
Massively in heat, hears her elkhound lover
Yelp on the hill and will not heel;
While under the weir the phlegmatic crayfish,
Gnome of these waters, ponderously grapples his viscid consort,
All fever aslake . . .

    Only myself,
Stooping to fathom his meaning here,
Know the tightening nerves . . .

What his time portends
I dare not guess. But much or little,
Brief or prolonged, in this recondite presence
I am favored in my life—honored in my being,
Illumined in my fate. As hieratic gesture
He sounds the death-pang of abnegation,
Witness to the world.

Segregate,
Wrenched out of context, bearing the suppressed
Restlessness of all disjunction, subsumed
In the abstract dimension this bloodlife abhors—
Out of time, out of season,
Out of place and out of purpose—
Ineluctable pariah, he burns in my dream
And calls me from sleep.

Who am hardly surprised
To find by the water his scattered remains
Where the racoons flung him: tore gill from fin,
Devoured the life-sustaining flesh, and left in clay
The faint skeletal imprint—as fossil
Etched in stone spans time like myth—
The glyph of God.

from The Masks of Drought

Cutting the Firebreak

Mowing the east field under the ridge
I wade the wind. The bent-rib scythe found rusting in the barn
Swings in the sun; the ancient blade of my wife's great-grandfather,
Drawn from the dust of seventy years, riots in the grass.

"They don't make 'em like this old gull anymore!" cackled the smith,
Hunched above his spectral grindstone,
Shouting across the howl of iron and the fleer of sparks.
He paused, spat on the blade, wiping off rust. In the sudden silence
The wedding band he wore on his finger chimed fine steel.
Cocking his head like a listening bird he snatched up a file and rapped
     again.
"Hear that hum in her spine, that tone when she shivers?"
He barked harsh laughter. "Old timers
Got a name for it." Turning, he cut the power,
Stepped down from the bench. *They call it*
The moan of death!"

                    And that hunger
Vibrates up the crooked stock as the grass reels.
I feel it hum in my arms; stroke on stroke
It sings in my shoulders; my collarbone
Rings to the pulse of it, the ravenous steel;
And I swing with it, made one with it,
Wheeling among the standing fern, goat-footed,

217

Trampling tall bracken, ruthless, the radiant flowers:
Iris, wild orchid, leopard lily—
The flush and shimmering splendor of life!

And then the honing: whetstone and steel
Kiss each other, they crave it so.
They lick their lips greedily together,
Like reckless lovers, or as the whore mouths the man.
I have to pull them apart.

                    The mad scythe
Hisses in the vetch, a snake denied, moans in the yarrow.
Whumph! Whumph! Oh, the grunt of lovers biting each other,
Stroke on stroke coupling through hell. It makes the sex
Growl in my groin to call them down, wild iris, lily,
The moan and the shudder. All the women in my life
Sprawled in the weeds—drunk in death.

Rattlesnake August

A rainless winter; week on week sun edging the hills,
And the frost's grey grip.

                    Summer broke dry,
A tightness of heat clenched the sterile coast, a fierce parching.
No fog fended the light; a threat of fire
Stung the rustling air. By midsummer's moon
Leaves littered raw earth.

                    Then late one dusk
Our Labrador bitch slogged home half lame,
Bleeding a little under the jaw, but we thought nothing of it:
Likely stuck on a thorn.

                    Morning found her prostrate,
The head hugely swollen, the throat hemorrhaging blood.
"Snakebite," said the vet, "and she's too far gone.
Tonight she will die."

                    We stared at each other.
Rattlesnakes in Big Creek canyon? Unheard of.
But the vet shook his head. "This God damned drought
Forces them down from their mountain dens
To creek water. We've known places this year
No snake's ever been seen in before,
And we're not done yet."

Now, with night dropping,
We sit in the hot unnatural silence,
Awaiting the friendly scratch at the door
We know will not come. This loss is a wound,
Tearing the sensitive fabric of our life, and it aches in us.
We think of the snake out there in the dark,
Lurking, the vibration of evil,
Coiling under the roots of trees,
Alive beneath stones, listening.

I see tears blind your eyes.
Tonight, I know, you will tear my snake-totem
Down from the wall, and burn it, bitterly,
Your lips moving, your eyes blue ice.

I do not begrudge it: your way is best.

For two themes contend here: the loss and the menace,
Double pang of the twisted heart.
We braced for disaster, a vast conflagration,
A holocaust borne on an eastern draft sweeping down to the sea,
Burning homesites and bridges, driving the coastal population
Out onto the roads.

It has yet to happen.
Rather, this subtle insinuation,
Gliding secretly into the warm nest
To spit venom.

Because sunspots
Distantly flare on the fountain of fire

Must something displace, hit at man's life,
Take his friend and companion?
Whatever he loves, be taken, must go?

I leave the table, step out under stars,
Smelling dryness in the air. And death,
The presence of death.

                      Lurker in the dark,
Where are you?

               Harried by heat,
Possessed of a taut desperation, the serpentine itch,
Driven down from some cool commodious hole higher up,
He descends, seeking water, water,
Raw slake for his thirst.

For he, too, loves life. He, too,
Craves comfort, smells it cunningly
Out. And when Fate accosts—
Licks his lip and stabs back.

Kingfisher Flat

A rustle of whispering wind over leaves,
Then the stillness closes: no creek-music,
No slurred water-sound. The starved stream
Edges its way through dead stones,
Noiseless in the night.

         I feel your body
Restless beside me. Your breathing checks
And then resumes, as in a moment of dream
The glimpsed image, mutely desired but scarcely believed,
Fades and revives.

        In the long drought
Impotence clutched on the veins of passion
Encircles our bed, a serpent of stone.
I sense the dearth in you also,
The bane that is somehow mine to impose
But yours to endure—cohibition of the blood,
Flaw of nature or defect of the soul—
Dry turning of leaves, cessation of desire,
Estrangement gripped in the roots of hair,
And around the loins, like a fine wire,
The cincture of nerves.

        I think of the Fisher King,
All his domain parched in a sterile fixation of purpose,
Clenched on the core of the burning question
Gone unasked.

Out in the dark
The recumbent body of earth sleeps on,
Silent as dust, incognizant. Many a moon,
Many a withering month will she weary
Ere the black knight of storm whirls out of the West,
Churns from the turbulent fosse of the sea,
Assaults the shore, breaches the continental slope
And takes her, his torrential force
Stripping the iron zone of chastity
Down from her thighs, drenching belly and breasts,
All the pores of her famished body
Agape—

Oh, wife and companion!
The ancient taboo hangs over us,
A long suspension tightens its grip
On the seed of my passion and the flower of your hope.
Masks of drought deceive us. An inexorable forbearance
Falsifies the face of things, and makes inflexible
The flow of this life, the movement of this love.
What prohibitive code stiffens the countenance,
Constricts the heart? What fear constrains it?
And whose the blame?

Enough.
There is no need now, nor ever was,
For the ghastly rote of self-accusation
Scrupulosity enjoins. To find a new mate
Were nothing difficult for one so young, so lovely.

But something other, more inscrutably present,
Obtains here, possessing us, cohesive in spirit,
Divisive in the flesh—the lordly phallus
Never again to joust in the festive lists of love,
Quench its ardour in the uterine fens,
Assuage your cry?

          Myth and dream
Merge in a consanguinity of kind,
Fuse the soul's wild wish and the hunger of the race
On the body's pang.

          But something forbears.
Like Merlin and Niniane, bound in a fatefulness
That set them aside, wisdom and delight
Crucified in bed, polarized on the stretched extreme
That made them one, we twist our grievous fingers together
And stare in the dark.

          I hear quaking grass
Shiver under the windowsill, and out along the road
The ripe mallow and the wild oat
Rustle in the wind. Deeper than the strict
Interdiction of denial or the serpentine coiling of time,
Woman and earth lie sunk in sleep, unsatisfied.
Each holds that bruise to her heart like a stone
And aches for rain.

Bride of the Bear

We camp by a stream among rugged stumps
In logged-over country. No tree shelters our bed.
In the year-long drought gripping the Sierras
There is now no snow, and the night is warm.
After our fog-haunted coast the air at this height
Seems weightless, without substance, almost clairvoyant.
Luminous stars, low overhead, look into our lives.
At ground level the campfire
Dapples the stumps, throws fitful shadows,
Guttering the dark.

                    We drink late wine.
Arriving at dusk we had pitched camp quickly,
Eaten nervous supper. For a ranger going out
Warned of bear sign, and a wrangler behind him
Showed packs ripped open, bacon gorged. Seeing it
We prudently stashed our food in the jeep,
Gathered firewood, branch and root,
And built up the blaze. Fumbling through our gear
My hand touched in passing the great bearskin
Carried in from the coast, belated wedding gift
Brought along to delight you, a savage pelt to throw down by the fire,
Barbaric trophy in a mountain lair—but here,
In the actual presence, in bear country,
Furtively concealed: discreet hibernation
In the cave of the car.

When the blaze dies down
I step out of its circle to fetch more wood
Against the presences of night. Standing in the dark
I look wondering up at those luminous orbs,
Hovering like moths just out of reach, preternaturally intense.
I sense around me the ghosts of slain trees,
Nude giants, slaughtered under the axe,
Pitching down from the slopes, the prone torsos
Hauled out with engines. Listening, I hear the famished creek
Drain west, a gurgle in a gravel throat,
Gasping.

Back by the fire
You have fallen asleep, dazed with wine,
Curled by bright embers on living fern.
I lace a clutch of twigs on the coals
And in the spurt of flame see gooseflesh
Stipple your arm. Under the mellowing influence of wine
My nerves loosen, and I dismiss caution.
I fetch from the jeep the great bearskin
And draw it across you, then fondly step back to admire my care.
But what have I wrought that my own hand shaped
Yet could not forestall? Oh, most inadvertently
I have folded you in the bear's huge embrace,
A hulking lover, the brute body enveloping you,
Massively yours.

You snuggle happily under it, sighing a bit,
The moan of a fretful satisfaction breathed from your deeps.
Is it wine on your lips that reddens them,
Or something deeper, in the bear's hug,

There, below the heart, a more elemental zone
At the body's base?

        I cannot tell.
But whatever it is it wantons your mouth,
And your mouth mocks me: inviting and denying,
The enigma of desire. I think, So be it.
Thus have I made you
Bride of the bear.

        And thinking it,
The night chill shivers me, a sudden *frisson,*
The languor of wine possessing me.
I feel surge through my veins
The madcap days of our courtship,
Crazy monk and runaway girl,
Panting in discovery, goading each other on,
Wildly in love.

        You stir in the bearskin.
Has memory touched you, two minds drenched in wine
Seeking each other through the cavern of sleep
Along the ancient line, the tendril of desire?

Drugged in dream you turn heavily. That nubile litheness
No longer is yours. But something better lives on in its place,
A mature abundance filling your flesh, the bloom of full life.

I, greybeard, nurse my drink and suck my pipe,
Watching the stars expire.

Now you turn,
Lifting your dream-drenched face to the light,
Still sunken in sleep, the wantonness
Splashed like wine on your parted lips.
Stiffly, raised on one elbow, you fumble at your blouse,
The heat under the animal pelt
Oppressing you. When your hand succeeds,
I see the naked globes of your breasts
Flash back the fire.

Bride of the bear.

Gazing up the dark I watch the stars
Cross the verge that shuts midnight from dawn
To walk down the west. Whatever happened to time?
When we pulled down our packs
The night lay before us. Now, in another hour,
Night is no more.

Somewhere out there
The ubiquitous beast, gorged on raw bacon,
Sleeps off his jag.

Raising your head
You look dazedly about, dimly comprehending,
Then sink back to sleep.

             Around the campfire
The ghosts of slain trees look over us.
Out of the eastern peaks, traced now with light,
The dawn wind whispers. The starved stream
Gropes through the stumps.

Spotfire

A single cap pistol,
Found on a shelf in a local market,
Left over from the Fourth.

Bought with his carefully hoarded coin
It hangs in his hand,
Cradled home through the heat.

Whipped from the hip,
Snapped fast, multiple explosions
Shatter the calm, break
The lazy afternoon.

He cocks and fires,
Cocks and fires,
The solitary sport of the only-begotten.

Round the corner of the house
He twists and slithers,
Fleeing bandits,
Then down across the creek
And up the other side.

Behind a fallen log
He flops on his belly,
Himself now the bandit, picks off
The converging posse.

Plunging back to the creek,
Bullets zinging about his head,
He makes his getaway,
Disappears down the road.

◆

A half-hour later
I stand in the yard of the Kingfisher Flat,
In the late light,
Barefooted, gazing leisurely about,
Smelling the air of approaching autumn,
The rare tang of fall,
Before drifting indoors
To mix the first drink.

Suddenly my eye, attracted upslope,
Catches color, a bright blaze,
Fire crackling up the skewed log.

"What the hell . . ."

I grab up a bucket, yelling to my wife.
She comes out the back, wondering,
Sees fire sharp on the hill
And her face blanches.

I race for the creek,
Aghast, bucket in hand.
There is hardly water,
But somehow I scoop it,

Half a pail at best,
And climb the steep slope,
Twisting and slipping,
My feet bleeding.
Where an eight-year-old kid
Scampered like a chipmunk,
I can hardly crawl.

Just in time I reach it,
The climbing fire,
And the water dashes it down.

Sliding back to the creek
I hit hard. My wife,
Standing slipper-deep in muck,
Hands another bucket,
Full and slopping over,
And I start the crawl back.

Now the boy shows up out of nowhere,
Running scared, grabbing pails,
Tin cans, fruit jars,
Anything to hold water.
Suddenly beside me,
He sloshes burning punk.

> Three trips and it's out,
> The blaze quenched.

We stand in the creek, the three of us,
Panting, thoroughly frightened,

Looking up at the hill,
The tangled thicket,
Mountain brush, tall standing timber,
Looking up the long half-mile of hillside above us,
And thinking:

>   Beyond it the range,
>   The crackling heat of fire-prone September,
>   And beyond that the State . . .

Incredulously staring, hardly daring to ponder
What a minute or two more
Must surely have meant.

(Who would have thought
The paper cap of a toy pistol
Could ignite the world?)

Breathing gratitude to God
For deliverance, the spared moment,
The sudden reprieve.

                    ◆

Two days later the episode is fading,
But what is etched in my mind
Is the glob of fire in the late light,
Orange red, the flames licking up,
A burning core of intensity,
Like the essence of a giant fruit,
As if we were being shown,
Through a slit in the skin,

The fiery inside:
A hole in the surface
To another dimension—

                    As if suddenly
Through the film of the earth
A flame stuck out its tongue,
Licking greedily,
Exposing all the impacted fire
Compressed at its heart.

And I fix my sight on it, my eyeball
Glued to the glory hole of a blast furnace,
Shaken by the intensity within,
The terror, a fury
Utterly belied by the inert scruff,
The thick vegetation
Masking the hill.

            It is crisis
Makes intensity intense.
Reality real.

            Place consequence in the scales
And watch the pans shiver.

Put fire and death,
Guilt and mortality
In the obsessive choice
And feel the nerves tighten.

I have seen my heart's fate
Shaped in the balance,
And known what I am.

But does *he?*

      His cap pistol
Is contraband till wet weather,
And he truly knows why.

            But is knowing
            Enough? Is knowing
            Ever enough?

I look up above at what might have been,
What fate just missed,
Black char climbing the sky,
Ten thousand acres of smouldering ash.

Somewhere, in the interstices of the self,
Like molten lava at the earth's core,
The principle of existence
Possesses its essence,
Primal, dangerous, unpredictable.
Out of our wayward impulses
It flashes and breaks free.

And I whisper:

             Lord, may what has been learned
Be learned in depth.

             For him.
For me.

The High Embrace

They stand in the clearing of Kingfisher Flat,
Twin giants, *sequoia sempervirens,* the ever-vernal,
And take in the arms of their upper branches
The last light crossing the bench-ridge west,
Sinking toward dusk.

                    Standing between them
I look up the double-columned space to the soaring crown,
Where those red-ribbed branches clasp each other in a high embrace.
For hundreds of years they have stood here, serenely apart,
Drinking clear creek water through sequaceous pores,
Feeling the flake of mountains sift chalkstone gravel about their boles,
Watching giant grizzlies scoop gravid salmon on the spawning bars
        below,
And tawny cougars stalk for fawns in their leaf-dappled shade.
They heard the kingfisher chirr his erratic intemperate cry,
While over their tops the slow-wheeling condors circled the sun,
Drifting south to their immemorial roosting ledges in the Los Padres
        peaks.
And they felt the demon of fire lick its running tongue up their shaggy
        skin
And not flinched, scorched but unscarred in the long warfare,
The stress-tension shaping fuel to fire,
The life-flux of their kind.

                    Tonight,
In the heat of the drought, we will forsake our bed,
Shutting the house-presence out of our thought,

Taking our respite in the open air. We will muse late,
And lay ourselves down by fir-bark embers,
Under the cape of the twin redwoods, swept back in time
A thousand years when this coast nurtured its kind—
The great beasts, the towering trees, the bird-flight migrations,
The shy coastal tribes. And in the sea-troughs of sleep
Our dreams will mirror the world above
Where stars swim over, and shadow the bloodstream's sibilance,
All through the foliage of the flesh, its fern-like fronds.

Up there above me the last light
Filters in as through stained glass windows,
Diffuse, glowing in the lofts of the upper branches,
Radiant and soft. And the mystery of worship
Descends on me, out of those far fenestrations.
And the God-awe, wake-wonder, envelops me,
Between the monumental straightness of columns
Bearing the sky, illuminate zone, twin towers
Conjoined above, clasped in the high embrace,
The soaring arch.

                    And the face of my son
Dawns between the gigantic boles
As he runs to meet me. And I ask in my heart
The graciousness of God, that he may grow in their presence,
As the tan-oak grows, as the fir-tree and fern,
As the chipmunk and the jay shelter under their span.

And I invoke their mystery of survival,
That the lightning-shattering years,
And the raw surge of fire,

May skim but not scar him—
As they themselves are scathed but unscarred—
Through the skip years of his childhood
And the leap years of his youth.

Make over our heads, then, the high embrace,
Like a blessing, the numinous descent, faith-fall,
Out of the heights, the leaf-light canopy,
The lofts of God, induplicate,
A gift regiven, the boon bestowed.

Stone Face Falls

Sheer naked rock. From the high cliff-cut
Straight falling water. Caught halfway down in a stone socket
It checks, boils over, then widens as it drops,
Snaking dreamily into the rockpool below.
Many months back it roared in flood;
Now, in the grip of drought, Big Creek the brawler,
Tamed and gentled, takes this pitch like a gliding dancer,
A shimmering sleeve against dark waterstains,
Storm-trek of the past.

                    We have come,
The two of us, in the white heat of noon,
To bathe at the fall-foot, a lambent pool
Under the salmon-stopping cliff.
We are struck by silence, the reduction of force,
Recalling those thunderous torrents of the past,
When the wild cataract drove everything before it,
Generating in its plunge a saturating gale,
Sopping a man a hundred feet below,
Drenched to the eyes in stinging spume.
But now, in the drought, the diaphanous film
Ripples down the rock, maidenly, a silken
Scarf, the veil of a bride, as virginal
And as lovely.

                Over our heads the great stone face
Juts from the gorge, a chief's visage hewn in raw granite,
Staring north, gazing down the long south-trek of his people,

Ten thousand years from the Bering Strait.
And the mystery keeps, the indomitable spirit
Guarding the secret where the water pulses,
The source, the slowed rhythm at the timeless center,
The heartbeat of earth.

I lower my gaze.
You are standing under the waterfall, nude, your body
An ivory wand against the seamed granite.
It is gleaming there, wreathed in water,
Breasts erect. The woman belly
And the female thighs
Shine in a shimmering ripple of lace,
The circling stream.

I move to meet you.

Suddenly a kingfisher swoops between.
In midflight he sees us, veers sharply,
Utters a sudden electrifying screech,
The ineluctable tension cruxed at the heart of things
Splitting his beak, the mystery
Out of which life springs and from which it passes.
Three times he circles, skirling his fierce
Importunate cry, then climbs the thermal,
The lazy updraft transcending the falls,
And disappears up the canyon.

You hold out your arms.

Dropping my clothes
I enter the pool,
Wade the ripple to where you stand.

It is the longest walk—
Out of the glacial
Past, through the pulsing present,
Into the clenched
Future—man to woman
Through time-dark waters.

                    Far ahead,
Beyond the stone face of the falls,
The cry of the kingfisher
Pierces the noon.

Spikehorn

The yearling buck, shot through the lungs,
Made it out of the brush and halfway to the stream
Before he fell. The illegal hunter
Never followed through. What dropped in the meadow
Died where it lay, unnoticed by any save two red bulls
Fenced in that field.

> The following day
A great black bird rose up when we came,
Lurched clumsily off, the wings made for soaring
Baffled now in this hemmed enclosure,
This deep forest field.

> Late that night
The coyotes found him. We heard from afar
The yelping chorus, clamoration of the feast,
High sung litany to the winnowing of time,
The brevity of life.

> Early next morning
The great bird was back with a dozen others,
A vulturine horde. Ghouls out of hell
They perched on the carcass, angling each other out
At the plucking, obscenely gobbling
The riddle of gut.

Our abrupt arrival
Sent them hissing aloft to circle and alight,
Teetering and balancing on the tall fir tops,
Refusing to abrogate their ancient
Prerogative, their ancestral place
At the sharing of the kill.

Two days later
The sentinel bulls stood over the torn and scattered remains,
Bellowing, lugubriously lowing, solemnly lamenting
The passing away of all slotted-hooved kind,
Mourning the death of their nimbler comrade,
Little cousin of the woods.

We paused there,
Disbelieving, and spoke to them as best we could.
They stared back, uncomprehending, not to be consoled.
Chagrined, we trudged on.

The following weeks
Left nothing much but a chewn shinbone and a scrap of hide.
No birds in the sky, no movement in the woods.
Nothing but the sparse pasture, the two red bulls
Placidly cropping the lank cover,
An emptiness in the air.

Then the changing year
Brought a leaf-flurry. Equinoctial rains
Replenished the earth. In the body-print of the buck
The first green grass quickened the bronze.

And we said:
The cycle is complete,
The episode is over.

But the silence that hung about that place
Was haunted, the presence of something anciently ordained,
Where we, unwitting acolytes, with the birds and the bulls
Enacted its rite: there in the immemorial clearing,
The great listening mountain above for witness,
The sacrificial host between the river and the woods.

Sixty Five

I stand in the center of a twilight field,
Distantly circled by dark woods,
But the woods hold no fear.

                    The meaning
Turns on an emptiness of space, of vague half-light,
The shadowless dusk beyond sundown.

                              My awareness
Is clear, the sense of subsistent identity
Distinct and whole. But there is nothing to apprehend,
Nothing save the circling space
And the weightless air.

                    What comes home
Is the total absence of force, the suspension of power,
Any capacity to *make*. Not paralysis,
Rather the dispersal of focus, as if the spirit
Retained unimpaired its powers of perception,
But the counter-thrust of brute causation,
Or the dramatic synthesis of form,
Have ineluctably passed.

I think:
This is the ghost-state—to behold reality
But not longer affect it. Soon comes the clinging
To what is no more, the ineffectual
Fumbling of the shards of experience,
Like King Arthur's ghost,
Dabbling his hands in Dozmare pool,
Groping the memory of a fabulous sword
That once was his all.

                I awake in chagrin,
Curled in a foetal suspension, afloat in time,
Hugging a sense of enigmatic loss.
A pulsation of pain, relinquishment
Of all the incisive forms I stood yet to create,
Drifts through me. Not the pang of death,
For death holds no terror. Rather,
The passing of rapacious joy, that appetitive
Sensuality and intellective thirst
Our slaking of which yields all we know
Of basal impulse: all we can keep
In heaven, or all we can hug
In hell: the signal
Instinct, the sovereign spirit,
The sceptral mind.

Danse Macabre

The place is public—a thronged station
Or perhaps the lobby of a large hotel.
Someone I know approaches, friend or acquaintance,
Dimly recalled but not clearly seen, his line of advance
Tangential to mine.

                    Who?

I will know him later for my very self,
That heron-like hunch of my Waldport years, but now
Unrecognized. No face and no name,
Nor has he yet noticed me.

                    I step aside,
Averting my gaze, and quicken my pace.
It is this evasion that sets me directly on course
Toward a man and a woman sitting casually by.
Turning my head I make to deflect again,
But before I can follow, the woman, rising,
Steps into my path. She will not be put off.

I check my stride. As I do
She lifts up her head, hooded, the cowl
Framing her face.

No face—a gaping skull,
Nor bones dry from the tomb.
Rather, bluish white, glistening, tatters of flesh
Still clinging her jaws—butcher's bones
Housewives lug home for dog-gnaw.

Taken aback
I half turn aside, but before I can dodge
She slips away, off toward the man,
Laughing, her face hidden now,
But her voice provocative.

Suddenly I seize her.
Under the cloak she is supple and firm,
Pulsing with life. I pull her to me,
Amorous, crush her in my arms
While she laughs and struggles.

I jerk awake.
I am clasping the recumbent body of my wife.
She is fast asleep, faced from me,
And I press against her.

Sensing arousal
She stirs her hips, languidly, still deeply asleep,
Too lost in the wonder of her own myth
To waken to mine.

And I lie listening,
Harkening the changing rhythm of my life,

The hope in the horror of the yet-to-be:
What the dream denotes.

                  As the ringing bell
Sounds in its knell the certitude of deliverance
From the sorrow it extols, so the eternal,
Haunting the instances of mutilation,
Chimes the measure of the unconceived.

Reaper

Winter's wake: week after week the sopping northwesters
Soaked the coast. When May, bedraggled, finally limped in,
The liberated sun sent the grass knee-high
And thick as cat's fur. Taking up the scythe put by last summer
I started to mow.

              This morning, honing the blade,
A spasm shook me—the Parkinson's reflex.
Struggling for balance I stumbled, fell forward,
Dropping scythe and hone to free my hands and break my fall.
But the crooked stock counterbalanced the blade,
Cat-quick, flipping the long point up and back.
Steel struck my face as I fell on it,
Drove into my cheek along the jaw,
And stuck there. Down on my knees I struggled with it,
And when it broke free blood gushed from the gash,
Drenching my beard.

              I staggered indoors,
Raining red on the floor, and yelled to my wife,
"Susanna! Come quick! I fell on my scythe!"
Who came wondering from the bedroom,
"Fell on your side?" then spotted the blood and ran to me.
Wrapping a towel round my lacerated jaw
She got me to the car and into town before I could grouse.

But when I badmouthed my lot the doctor would have none of it:
"Count your blessings, man. It was very close.
A little to the left and a bit lower down
Would have split your mouth or slit your throat.
Consider yourself in luck."

                    Back home, luckily unlucky,
I regard my image in the looking glass
And I say to myself: What a way to go!
The mad scythe, cutting the firebreak ten years back,
All the women in your life laid low with the flowers,
Now turns on you. Drunk in death
Would you hug them to your heart?
The world at large would receive your demise
With grave satisfaction, struck by its fitness,
Savoring the rough justice, the karmic violence
That never quits, those howling Erinyes
Pursuing vengeance down the rooftree of the world.

It is not so—not yet anyway. In the springtime dusk
I feel no fear, and I whisper,
"Death, you darling! Come quick if you love me!
Tease me not, brazen hussy! Think rather
We have pledged our troth in violent verse
And not flinched.

                 Today you kissed me
Almost on the mouth. I know by this
You have readied the place, prepared the bed,
Where breast to breast we will slake desire
Each of the other, and leave this life
Enjoined."

252

The Blood of the Poet

My first remembrance: the yard of our earliest
Selma sojourn, corner of Logan
And Gaither streets, on the east side of town.

The occasion: a bevy of neighborhood children
At play on the lawn, myself among them,
And no doubt my sister, though I can't recall her.
Certainly my brother is still a mewling babe-in-arms,
Which goes far to explain the conspicuous
Absence of my mother; she is seldom without us.

Instead, a couple of neighbor women, standing by in supervision,
Complete the scene. No men around. At so early a date
In the new century, the nursery syndrome precludes it.

Suddenly the lazy summer stillness is shattered by a scream.
It is my own. I have stabbed my foot on a piece of broken bottle
Hidden in the grass. How long it has lain there,
Like a serpent coiled to strike, no one can say,
Least of all a two year old kid,
Sheltered by his mother from accidental mishap
Or archetypal malice, till the rude day dawns,
To find him unready.

Heedless as a pup
I frolicked with my kind, ecstatic in that animal
Abasement of the self before the power of the pack,
Till the mother's untoward absence
Exposed the flaw, and in my child's
Fear-benighted reckoning the serpent
Found my foot.

Or did my foot
Find the serpent? In the cloudy womb of causation
Who nudges whom? Falling to the ground
I twist in terror at the seizure of my blood,
Shrieking to high heaven, bringing the scared children
And the alarmed adults crowding about me.

Someone fetches from the near back porch
A white enamelled basin, full and slopping over
With pure tap water—a household utensil
Familiar enough to the ubiquitous back porches
Of small town America; but this time it threatens.
Scrambling frantically up on my useless leg
I look wildly around for my mother. But when these sudden
Strangers seize my ankle and thrust in my foot,
I yell bloody murder.

But I quickly recover,
Brought up short by the awe-struck faces
Clustered about me. I blink back my tears,
Too paralyzed by pain to see what they see,

But too rapt in the grip of the simmering archetype
Not to feel what they fear.

                      Then my vision fixes.
For out of my fragile, fang-pierced foot
Pulses the wellspring of my fugitive blood,
A ribbon of red, unfurling in the pellucid water,
Beautiful in its sanguinary loveliness,
Solemnly performing its surrogate office,
The changing of water to wine, as earnestly intense
As the serenade of life or the swan-song of death.

Years later, under the rubric of the castration complex,
I will read it as the sleeve of a lady's favor
Tangled on his helmet where her knight lay dead,
(Slain in defense of her precious honor)
But eased by the solace of the jongleur in her bed.

So does the symbol, latent in the stuff of life,
Reconstitute its truth. But for now,
It spells only terror: this it is that fastens every eye,
Victim and lookers-on alike, in the portentous drama
Unfolding here.

                   So the wound bleeds on
Picking up passion as it flows, compounding its enigmatic purpose
Till that humble and hallowed icon, the basin,
That once on Golgotha caught the veritable
Gore of God, source of its numinous efficacy, only to become,

By virtue of what grave default, the World Ill's
Stinking bucket of blood?

                    But the ills of the world,
By God's clear injunction, are to be reckoned
Implicitly benign. His vivid signature, dazzlingly
Calligraphed on trees, rivers, rocks, buttes and benchlands,
The ordeal of life is the measure of its meaning.
Perdurably opportune, the hostages of pain
Never fail to envince the quantification of value
In the substance of the soul.

                    It will be roughly
Twenty more years before the tongue of this poet
Finds its true tenor. But the centrality of vision,
Which the presence of his peers, in their invincible naïveté,
Evoke within him, will, in God's good time,
Given the centrifugal passion at the heart of things,
Confirm his destiny.

                    Nor do I cry anymore,
But watch with amazement the limpidity of water
Undergo its savage metamorphosis,
To become before my astounded eyes,
Stunned in the existential verge of the Real,
A token of the poet's inimitable
Credential—his consecrated blood.

Afterword

Under the Sign of Woman

by Albert Gelpi

I

In reviewing *The Crooked Lines of God*—the first volume that William Everson published as the Dominican monk Brother Antoninus—Kenneth Rexroth, the poet-critic who served as catalyst and iconoclastic mage of the poets of the San Francisco Renaissance during the 1940s and 1950s, described the poems as manifesting "the ultimate, agonized sincerity that makes for a great truly personal style." A couple of years earlier, when he was introducing his circle of poets to a national audience in a special edition of *The Evergreen Review*, he had singled out Everson/Antoninus as "probably the most profoundly moving and durable of the poets of the San Francisco Renaissance" and had gone on to say: "His work has a gnarled, even tortured honesty, a rugged unliterary diction, a relentless probing and searching, which are not just engaging but almost overwhelming. . . . Anything less like the verse of the fashionable quarterlies would be hard to imagine." Rexroth had in mind the academic reviews dominated by the New Criticism, but the qualities that make Everson/Antoninus one of the most powerful and engrossing poets since the mid-century set him off even more categorically from the postmodernist, poststructuralist modes currently prevailing in literary quarterlies and reviews.

I shall return to the question of Everson's place in modern American poetry in the second, more strictly literary section of this essay, but here I want to take up Rexroth's emphasis on the personal and autobiographical aspect of the work so as to relate the poems in this selection to the dramatic course of the poet's life. For Everson's work, especially starting from the fifties, resists the distinction between art and life as

257

strenuously as the "confessional poetry" published by Robert Lowell, W. D. Snodgrass, Sylvia Plath, and others (most of them, in one way or another, in Lowell's poetic orbit) during roughly the same period. It is a Romantic, and particularly an American, axiom that the local is the universal and the individual self is the representative, so that the poet enacts an agon at once personal and collective, and the autobiographical grounding gives the work both its distinctive character and its terms of representation. (For a full-length biography, see Lee Bartlett's *William Everson: The Life of Brother Antoninus* [New Directions, 1988], from which much of the factual information, though not necessarily the interpretation, in this essay derives.)

Born on September 10, 1912, in Sacramento, California, William Everson was the second child of three and the older son. His parents were a Norwegian immigrant and a rural Minnesota woman of German-Irish descent fifteen years younger than he. Everson's father Louis held various jobs, including typesetter and printer, as he moved around the country, but it was his native talent as a self-taught musician that got him the position as band-master in the town of Selma, celebrated in one of his locally popular songs, "Selma, Home of the Peach." In this little farm community near Fresno in the San Joaquin Valley, one of the most productive agricultural areas in California, Everson grew up, and those roots remain deep in the poet.

His paternal grandfather, besides being a shoemaker in Norway, had founded and presided over an evangelical Protestant sect called the Iversonians. (In the old country the family spelled the name with an initial "I," and it is pronounced still with a long rather than short "E" sound.) The early poem "Bard" expresses the poet's abiding sense that the diction and syllabic texture of his language, as well as its rhythmic base and unmetered, heavily alliterative line, derive in large part from his Scandinavian and Germanic origins. Louis Everson rejected his father's fundamentalism for a free-thinking and skeptical indifference in religious matters. But Francelia Herber Everson remained religious even after abandoning the Catholicism in which she was reared to marry the divorced Louis, and the children were brought up as Christian Scientists. The son William recalls childhood, torn between his austere, authoritarian father and his loving and protective mother, as presaging the course of his life.

William was a withdrawn, brooding boy and an indifferent student at Selma Union High School, and attended Fresno State University erratically, for a semester in 1931 and then two semesters in 1934–1935, without completing a degree. But his life was slowly beginning to take its initial direction during his twenties. At Selma High he had fallen in love with Edwa Poulson. They wed in 1938 after an eight-year engagement, during which he had worked at various jobs, and he began married life by turning to the land and cultivating a vineyard of muscat grapes on a farm not far outside of town. By college age an agnostic like his father but unsatisfied by disbelief, Everson chanced upon a volume of Robinson Jeffers' poems on the library shelves at Fresno State in the fall of 1934. What he read on those pages precipitated his first conversion and made him simultaneously a pantheist and a poet. Those poems gave him, blinded and dumbstruck by their revelation, his own eyes and his own tongue. Responding to Jeffers' descriptive evocation of the divine but brute beauty of the sea and sky and shore of the Carmel coastline, Everson found transcendence in the vast distances, tumultuous skies, and fertile fields of his native San Joaquin Valley. The year after his discovery of Jeffers, and of himself through Jeffers, he published a paper-bound pamphlet of short poems called *These Are the Ravens*, partly at his own expense (as Whitman had done with the first editions of *Leaves of Grass*).

These poems and those that followed in *San Joaquin* (1939) and *The Masculine Dead* (1942)—see "We in the Fields," "August," and other poems which open this selection—show Everson intensifying and humanizing the erotic element in Jeffers' pantheism with the sexual mysticism he had absorbed from D.H. Lawrence, especially through Lawrence's poetry. But the dates of these books bracket the outbreak of the Second World War and America's entry into it. "Orion," the armed and phallic warrior, is the constellation hovering over poems like "October Tragedy" ("my first true poem" after reading Jeffers), "The Hare," and "Attila." The peace and exaltation of these early pantheist poems are crossed repeatedly by a tragic foreboding and impending violence that anticipated the hostilities that would also put Jeffers' pantheism to the incendiary test. Where Jeffers fulminated against the war and articulated a philosophy of "Inhumanism" that looked forward to the extinction of the human species as an aberrant biological violation of the sublime natural order, the draft-aged Everson faced a more difficult and painful choice. As the men of his generation went off to fight, he sought and was granted status as a conscientious objector, which exempted him from military duty but required service in a C.O. work camp. Opposition to what some would come to call, grotesquely and not even ironically, "the good war" required an unpopular and brave stand on principle, and from January 1943 to July 1946 Everson lived under quasi-military regulation, doing forest reclamation in Oregon, for most of that time at the Waldport camp, which also housed many other literary and artistic C.O.'s. There Everson published several thin volumes of pacifist poems—see "The Raid" (about Pearl Harbor) and "Eastward the Armies" in this volume—through the Untide Press, which he established with several associates at the camp. Everson's first venture into his father's old trade would lead to a printing career after the war that would make him one of the most admired book designers and hand-press printers in the country.

During these years of camp camaraderie and isolation from his wife, his marriage wrenched apart: in his absence Edwa had taken up her life with one of their close friends. Peace, when it came, found Everson wracked by the internal conflict he bared in the long poem "Chronicle of Division": alienated from a society exultant with victory while arming now for the Cold War, and uprooted as well from the land he had cultivated and the wife of his young manhood. "Sea," the long fifth and concluding part of "Chronicle of Division," stands as a momentous summing up of the lost past for a turn to an unknown and un-

certain future. Instead of returning to the San Joaquin Valley he was
drawn to the seacoast, not to Jeffers' Big Sur wilderness, but to Berke-
ley and San Francisco, by a trio of new associates: Rexroth and the
slightly younger Robert Duncan, both of whom he had been corre-
sponding with, and the poet-artist Mary Fabilli. The intersection be-
tween the Berkeley poets constellated around Duncan and the anarchist
group of artists constellated around Rexroth made for the San Fran-
cisco Renaissance, and Everson soon found himself a craggy, brooding,
solitary figure amidst all the heated discussion of postwar poetry and
politics.

And almost immediately he found himself passionately in love with
Mary Fabilli. Despite the loss of Edwa (or perhaps through that loss)
Everson had come to associate his destiny with the figure of the woman:
in his life as lover and wife, in his art as muse, and in his psychological
drama as the feminine aspect of his own identity that, he would learn
later, Jung called the anima. But long before he had read Jung, he was
invoking the "woman within" as the key to his selfhood. These lines
from the sequence "In the Fictive Wish," written after "Chronicle of
Division" and before he had met Mary, hymn union with the anima:

Wader,
Watcher by wave,
Woman of water;
Of speech unknown,
Of nothing spoken.

But waits.

And he has,
And has him,
And are completed.

So she.

Immediately upon the first encounter with Mary, the woman within
seemed to have found the woman in his life, and Everson began *The
Blowing of the Seed*, a spring sequence celebrating their new life to-

gether: "I move to meet you in a greening time," he sings in the "Epilogue." They married in June, 1948, and in her Berkeley house set up the huge Washington handpress, newly purchased, on which he printed a couple of exquisite books of his own design with her woodblocks as illustrations.

However, the strange and excruciating paradox is that their married life was to last only a year—not through any estrangement but, ironically, through their intense affinity. Mary was a Catholic in the toils of rediscovering her spirituality, and Everson was drawn into an inner quest of his own out of empathy with her and out of dissatisfaction with "my Jeffersian pantheism and my Lawrentian erotic mysticism" as an explanation of nature and self. Early in the marriage he began to attend Sunday Mass from time to time; he read St. Augustine's *Confessions* and other works on Catholic belief. Then at Christmas Midnight Mass, 1948, in San Francisco's cathedral, came the stupendous experience that subsumed the conversion of 1934 and redefined, psychologically and spiritually, all the terms of his life. He felt an understanding of the Incarnation as the central mystery of existence: not just God immanent in nature but God in the person of Jesus suffering mortality to transcendence. The dawning of that epiphany seemed to offer "for the first time that synthesis of spirit and sense that I had needed and never found"; "that was the night I entered into the family and fellowship of Christ—made my assent, such as it was—one more poor wretch, who had nothing to bring but his iniquities."

The convert began to take formal catechetical instruction in Catholicism by April, and was baptized at St. Augustine's Church in Oakland in July, 1949, a month after separating from Mary. For such was their commitment that they both accepted as the wrenching consequence of their faith the separation required at that time by the Church's marital laws: not because of his marriage to Edwa (from which he could—and in due course would—obtain an ecclesiastical dispensation) but because of Mary's previous marriage. Everson had followed his spring poem to Mary with *The Springing of the Blade* (not included here), but

The Falling of the Grain, the poem he wrote in the autumn after his baptism, construes the harvest of their love as separation. The blown seed is displaced by the fallen ear of grain which, in the gospel trope, must die in the natural cycle for a springtime beyond the seasons. Several years later, in the prose memoir *Prodigious Thrust* (still unpublished except for a few excerpts) he would recount his conversion as an enraptured tribute to the graced inspiration of Mary Fabilli.

A selection of the poetry up to this point had appeared as *The Residual Years,* in 1948. Twenty years later in the monastery, Antoninus would gather under the same title all of Everson's poems from 1934 to 1948 as the first of three projected volumes of his life's work. But in 1949, adrift and alone at the end of his life with Mary, of his Guggenheim Fellowship, and of his close association with the San Francisco Renaissance, he did not yet know where his new life would take him. In the spring of 1950, he moved to an Oakland house run by the pacifist-socialist Catholic Worker movement of Dorothy Day to help provide food and shelter for the poor and homeless. One morning at Mass he "was seized by a feeling so intense as to exceed anything I had previously experienced . . . a feeling of extreme anguish and joy, of transcendent spirituality and of a great, thrilling physical character." The revelation, the mystical climax of his life, came from the tabernacle on the altar as "an intense invisible ray, a dark ray" whose impact, at once spiritual and erotic, possessed him totally and knocked him, dazed and exalted, to the floor of the church.

Even before this staggering moment he had been drawn to join a religious order. A year later, in June, 1951, Everson entered the Dominicans as a lay brother at St. Albert's Priory in Oakland and was given the monastic name Brother Antoninus. He would describe the visitation of the dark ray metaphorically in "The Encounter," and it is no exaggeration to say that, for the next twenty years and more, his life and his poetry would explore the incarnational mystery which we humans, self-divided between body and soul, experience through the tensions and revelations of what Everson/Antoninus calls "erotic mysticism."

The Crooked Lines of God (1959) contains the conversion poetry of the late forties and early fifties in a handsome edition designed by the poet. In the foreword he sees the poems as responding to the witness of a succession of saints: Augustine (in, for example, "The Screed of the Flesh"), Francis of Assisi (in "A Canticle to the Waterbirds"), the Spanish mystics John of the Cross and Teresa of Avila (in "Annul in Me My Manhood" and "A Canticle to the Christ in the Holy Eucharist"). By 1954, however, the poetic inspiration had dried up. Antoninus threw himself into the gargantuan project (never completed) of designing and printing on his handpress an edition of the Psalms in a new Latin translation, into writing *Prodigious Thrust*, the rhapsodic prose memoir of his conversion, and into trying out study for the priesthood. After a year's novitiate, he returned to his status as a lay brother but still faced a major block in his psychological, spiritual, and so poetic life. With the help of Fr. Victor White, the English Dominican theologian whose book *God and the Unconscious* undertook a reconciliation of Jungian archetypal psychology and Catholic theology, Antoninus achieved a breakthrough in 1956 by tapping into the unconscious and releasing its energies into expression.

The catharsis began with a dream in July, 1956, on the anniversary of his baptism. The first poem which emerged is the narrative poem *River-Root*, written during the fall of 1957 (partly in response to Allen Ginsberg's *Howl*). In the Afterword to *The Veritable Years* I called *River-Root* "the most sustained orgasmic celebration in English, perhaps in all literature," and it marks a major turning point in the poet's investigation of erotic mysticism. The book-length poem, available from Broken Moon Press, is represented here only by the introductory passage describing the gathering of the waters, which can stand sufficiently on its own. Though the monk displaced the subsequent narrative action of the poem from the Pacific coast to the American heartland on the banks of the Mississippi and cast it as the description of a night's love-making between a married Catholic couple, the extended and explicit account of the physical and anatomical details of intercourse, far from being prurient or pornographic, is necessary to ground and substantiate the intimation of sexual ecstasy as the Beatific Vision. In its most extreme and shocking moment, the procession of the Trinity becomes the kinetic drive within the sexual act. Antoninus subtitled *River-Root* "A Syzygy," the Jungian term for the reconciliation of opposites in the sublime process of individuation, and he takes the fictional child conceived at the poem's climax to announce his self reborn from the syzygy the poem achieves.

However, not surprisingly perhaps, the extraordinary afflatus of *River-Root* led quickly to a frightening descent into what Antoninus has described as his "dark night of the soul," recorded in the poems from 1957 to 1960 published in *The Hazards of Holiness* (1962). In poems like "Passion Week," "You, God," "I Am Long Weaned," "In the Breach," and "A Frost Lay White on California," the prevailingly short lines—end-stopped, heavily monosyllabic, harshly consonantal—stammer and gasp and spit out the tormented contention of body and spirit which the requirements of monastic celibacy intensified. Relief came, unexpectedly and paradoxically, through his meeting with a Mexican-American woman named Rose Moreno Tannlund, and by the early sixties he was writing what would evolve into the book-length "love-poem sequence" *The Rose of Solitude* (1967), perhaps his crowning poetic achievement.

In the narrative, played out through groupings of intense lyrics, the love between a monk and a woman as pious as she is passionate becomes, in Augustine's phrase, a "happy fault" which awakens a deepened sense of human fallibility and divine forgiveness. It is an old story of love and parting, but this frankly autobiographical exploration takes on an emotional and rhetorical power that is like nothing else in modern literature. In Antoninus' telling, Rose becomes the means of grace for him through her instinctual and loving adhesion to God's will, and as Rose becomes "the Rose" she assumes a symbolic and archetypal power beyond her personal self: the apotheosis of his anima and a Marian mediatrix of grace. The selections from the sequence in this volume provide sufficient narrative context for the two great long-lined canticles to her at the heart of the book: the exalted fusion of elemental imagery and theological abstraction in "The Canticle of the Rose" paired with the exclamatory litany of the title poem, "The Rose of Solitude." *The Veritable Years 1949–1966,* the second collected volume of the poet's life-work, is prefaced by a dedication to Mary Fabilli and concludes with the *Rose* sequence.

It is clear by now that, from "Chronicle of Division" and "In the Fictive Wish" through *The Blowing of the Seed* and *The Falling of the Grain* to *River-Root* and *The Rose of Solitude,* the decisive turns in Everson/Antoninus' poetic agon—and it has to be read as a *man's* psychodrama—transpire under the sign of woman. As he engages or invokes the Jungian archetypes more and more consciously, erotic mysticism tends to express itself in two complementary modes that open into and revert into each other, interpenetrating like the double helix or the cones in a gyre. In the mystical dimension the male learns from St. Teresa that "the soul is feminine to God" and experiences himself as the woman before Deity, himself (like Mary) the vessel for the Spirit's insemination. At the same time, in the material order he experiences God as woman (*"I am your woman,"* God says in "A Frost Lay White on California") under the aspect of the feminine: not just through nature but through the woman's incarnation of the Incarnation. Teresa's mysticism proves erotic; Mary's and Rose's eroticism proves mystical. One way and the other, the Virgin-Mother and her avatars play a more immediately mediatory role even than Jesus in Everson/Antoninus' imaginative life.

In 1964, with Rose's blessing, Antoninus took vows as a First Order Dominican and worked on the final sections of the *Rose* volume, which would be published in 1967. At the same time, his renewed dedication to the monastic life was put to the test by the passionate love he came to feel for Susanna Rickson, a young woman thirty-five years his junior who had been sent to him for counseling in the fall of 1965. *Tendril in the Mesh* celebrates their love, while seeking to mythologize it through the story of Persephone and Pluto, and to sacralize it by the invocation of the "dark God of Eros." However, where "The Canticle of the Rose" moved to transcendence, the chthonic, plutonic drive expressed in *Tendril* could, in the end and after several years' struggle, not be accommodated within the terms of monastic life. In December, 1969, Antoninus read the poem publicly for the first time at the University of California, Davis, and then told the stunned audience that he was leaving the Dominican Order to marry Susanna.

Everson moved with Susanna and her infant son Jude first to Stinson Beach, just north of San Francisco, and then to a firewatcher's cabin, deep in a canyon off Highway 1, but near enough to Santa Cruz for him to begin a ten-year stint in 1971 as Poet-in-Residence at the university there. The poems published in *Man-Fate* (1974) record the trauma of his break with monasticism and the struggle to recover autochthonous power through a series of ritual dream-visions of passage and survival. For the recursion to the earth in "The Narrows of Birth" brings him to the dark underworld of the psyche, where, weakened by the prodigal's guilt, he is forced to confront the judgment of the archetypal feminine and masculine. Only after facing the threat of castration by the mother in "The Narrows of Birth" and the malediction of the father in "The Black Hills" can he begin to assume his new role as mountainman, far from the monk's cloister, and undertake life with the woman, as he could not with Edwa or Mary or Rose, on her own ground.

While gathering the poetry of Brother Antoninus into *The Veritable Years* (Black Sparrow, 1978), volume two of his collected poems, Everson was already projecting a third volume as *The Integral Years*, because, after leaving the Order but never the faith, he saw his return to nature not as a reversion or regression to an earlier attitude, but rather as a deepened commitment to material creation through a specifically Christian-Incarnational sense of its power and mystery. The poems of *The Masks of Drought* (Black Sparrow, 1980) and its coda *Renegade Christmas* (1984), generously represented here, graphically re-create the topography of Everson's canyon, which he named Kingfisher Flat.

In these poems theology is now largely submerged in description and narration of the new-old husband's domestic life in the woods, but theological assumptions and implications inform the language of description and narration, so that the giant redwoods and the steep, densely thicketed hillsides, the creek flowing seaward from the falls upstream, the birds and animals and fish of Kingfisher Flat comprise a microcosm to express Everson's "integral" vision.

And to test it. The Romantic sense that (in Emerson's words) "the universe is the externization of the soul" directs us to read landscape as psyche; but here, as the title of the sequence indicates, Kingfisher Flat, magnificent and even sublime, but parched tinder-dry in the deadly drought of 1976–77, presents a psychological landscape gripped by the onset of age and impotence. By the end of the sequence the paralysis of the drought is released with the coming of the rains and, correspondingly, through twinned events: the mystical adumbration of God in "The High Embrace" of the sequoias paired (like Baucis and Philemon in ancient myth) beside the Eversons' cabin, and the erotic renewal of husband and wife under "the cry of the kingfisher" and the baptism of "Stone Face Falls." In this last poem Everson echoes T. S. Eliot's and Robert Lowell's invocation of the kingfisher and here has it emblemize the redemptive Christ-presence in the "serene agonization" (to recall the phrase from "In All These Acts" years earlier) of incarnational renewal. In its description of the assimilation of a dead buck back into the cycle of life-death-rebirth, "Spikehorn," the last poem in *The Masks of Drought*, recalls "In All These Acts" directly; however, the violent epiphany of the earlier poem is replaced here by meditative calm, ritual action, and liturgical language, invoking "the presence of something anciently ordained" in the "immemorial clearing" to consecrate this "sacrificial host between the river and the woods."

Meanwhile, at the University of California, Santa Cruz, Everson was teaching each year an immensely popular year-long course whose lectures were distilled into *Birth of a Poet* (1982), and was also conducting a workshop for undergraduate students on hand-press printing, which trained some of the best book designers and printers in the area. The crowning achievements of the Lime Kiln Press were two books honoring Everson's poetic fathers. *Granite and Cypress* (1975) brought together Jeffers' poems about Tor House, the stone residence and tower he built for his family in Carmel, on pages of hand-made paper so wide that Jeffers' lines could spill out their full length without breaking; *American Bard* (1982), illustrated by two woodcuts by Everson and decorated with red and blue initials, liberated the Preface to the 1855 *Leaves of Grass*, into poetry through Everson's intuitively right lineation of Whitman's heavy block-prose paragraphs into free verse.

The advancing symptoms of Parkinson's disease, first diagnosed in 1977, ended Everson's residence at the university in the early eighties, but, because the affliction has spared his mental and creative powers, he continues, with increasing physical difficulty, to write and, on special occasions, to give readings. *The Engendering Flood* (Black Sparrow, 1990) is the first book of the "autobiographical epic" to bear the title *Dust Shall Be The Serpent's Food.* These four cantos recount the stories of his parents and conclude with his conception. The subsequent cantos of a projected ten will climax with the poet's conversion to Catholicism.

"The Blood of the Poet," Canto 5 and the last completed so far, mythicizes his first memory of pain: cutting his foot at the age of two. In an audacious stroke of imaginative synthesis, Everson turns the pan of water turned wine-red with the boy's blood into an intimation of the man's vocation as a Christian poet: the transmutation of his life's suffering into the sacrificial and redemptive action of the Incarnation. For that reason, "The Blood of the Poet" is, appropriately, both the concluding poem in this volume and the title of the entire selection.

September 1992 marked an important milestone and a new turn of events. Everson's eightieth birthday was celebrated under the redwoods amidst dear and old friends, but soon thereafter he and Susanna separated. Nevertheless, perhaps the separation, painful as it was, confirmed a kind of reversion that was already in process. In "Steelhead," one of the poems of *The Masks of Drought*, he had seen himself suddenly not as the husband but as the "God-stoned monk" of Kingfisher Flat. In his canyon cabin there, Everson lives out what awaits him in his integral years—as before, within the sacrament of Nature and the sacraments of the Church, under the imaginative, at once the erotic and spiritual, sign of the woman.

II

In his introduction to *The Residual Years* (1968), Rexroth catalogued Everson's predecessors, from the Old Testament prophet Isaiah through the Romantic prophets Blake and Whitman to Lawrence and Jeffers, the pair of anti-Modernist prophets in the Modernist generation. Rexroth posited as the source of these poets' kinship and their poetic-prophetic empowerment the fact that they were all autochthons, rooted in their place and time so deeply that they spoke with the authority of the divine energy immanent in but transcendent to place and time. They were also, by choice and vocation, all solitary figures, even Whitman amidst a crowd on the Brooklyn Ferry, but they all felt impelled to speak to and for their people, for and in the name of God or Nature.

Years later, after Jeffers' death, Everson would recognize his first master in *The Poet Is Dead*, one of the great American elegies, in several editions of Jeffers' works (some from previously unpublished manuscripts), in the magnificent design and printing of *Granite and Cypress*, and in two groundbreaking critical studies, *Robinson Jeffers: Fragments of an Older Fury* (1968) and *The Excesses of God: Robinson Jeffers as a Religious Figure* (1988). Yet as younger poet, perhaps because of the power of this poetic father, Everson never played the filial disciple, seeking acknowledgement only once, and that unsuccessfully. Instead he avoided apprenticeship and preferred to maintain a safely independent distance from Jeffers, as later from all mentors, out of an ambivalence about the paternal authority he needed but resisted from the depth of his need. As a result, the long free-verse line that Everson developed out of Jeffers is characterized by a more immediate and convulsed emotional registration than Jeffers' line, and correspondingly by richly orchestrated rhythmic and aural harmonics and a dense syllabic texture that are all Everson's own. Where Jeffers' line seeks to expand into the open space of sea and sky, Everson's turns back on its own aural and emotional convolutions.

Nevertheless, Jeffers was indispensable to Everson in serving as his point of entry into the Romantic and post-Romantic prophetic tradition. And the idiosyncratic independence which let him maintain himself against Jeffers early on also allowed him after the war to ignore Rexroth's loud and oedipal rejection of Jeffers, and to resist taking Rexroth or any of his peers in the San Francisco Renaissance as literary models. In fact, his principal literary and philosophical debt to Rexroth was a deepened response to Lawrence, whose Whitmanian sense of the sexual mystery of the self and of nature Everson assimilated into his Jeffersian pantheism.

It was, therefore, through Jeffers and the Britisher Lawrence that Everson tapped into the autochthonous tradition of the American bard whose source was Whitman: all of them male poets who lived and wrote, in their different ways, under the sign of woman. Where Jeffers celebrated nature but abjured the self, Lawrence also celebrated the self, and in Everson's assimilation of both poets he found the two terms that he needed, and found them already incorporated in Whitman. Everson and Whitman came from opposite coasts and cultures, and Whitman was a city-man where Everson, like Jeffers, was and remains at heart a country-man. But, like Whitman and his other literary descendants, Everson is a visionary who seeks to conduct the transpersonal, supernatural power instinct in the bodily self and his particular American locale so as to allow it to break through and break out into a transforming sense of self and nature. What's more, Everson learned, initially through Jeffers' mediation, that the American language for conveying that vision sought the organic, open form and long, free-verse line that Whitman had devised as the literary means to reach out and draw in, to extend and enfold, to embrace and resolve the constituent parts into a microcosm of the constituting whole.

Among the poets of the San Francisco Renaissance, Robert Duncan frequently expressed his affinity with Whitman. But in fact his imagination was much more Modernist than Everson's, and Duncan's line evolved more directly from Pound's, in which the ideogrammic method sought to break not only the iambic pentameter, as Pound declared, but also to fracture Whitman's indiscriminate inclusiveness into (Pound's phrase) luminous details and (Williams' phrase) radiant gists. (Early in their friendship, Duncan sent Everson Pound's Imagist poems to read as a counterweight to Jeffers' excesses.) Rexroth was himself too close to the Modernists to follow Whitman any more than he could follow Jeffers; Lawrence was as far as he would go. Everson recalled that Rexroth labelled Duncan the "Dionysian aesthete" of the group and Philip Lamantia the "Dionysian surrealist," but Rexroth made it clear on several occasions that the Dionysian pantheist Everson was in many respects the closest to the notion of the bardic poet that Rexroth could never comfortably embrace for himself (Bartlett, pp. 92, 97).

What's more, in the late fifties the Whitmanian element was strengthened nationally by the sudden eruption of the Beats into the literary scene and locally by the Beat infusion into the San Francisco Renaissance through the frequent visitations of easterners like Allen Ginsberg and Jack Kerouac and through the relocation of poets like Michael McClure and Lawrence Ferlinghetti to the Bay Area. Where the poetic and prosodic adhesion of other open form poets, such as Gary Snyder and Denise Levertov and Robert Creeley, is immediately to Pound and, even more strongly, to Williams, the Beats' adhesion to Whitman is paramount. So it was altogether appropriate that Rexroth should feature Everson, by then Brother Antoninus, along with Kerouac and Ginsberg and Duncan in the issue of *The Evergreen Review* he edited in 1957 to proclaim the amalgamation of the Beats into the San Francisco Renaissance. Now we can look back and see that, in fact, Everson and Ginsberg stand, in the American tradition after Jeffers, as the most important contemporary inheritors of the Whitmanian position with its long free-verse line in counterdistinction to the late Modernist poetics of the Black Mountain poets and, more recently, in opposition to Postmodernist language-poetry. And Everson's work exhibits a more sustained power of vision and language, a broader range and variety, a greater capacity for development than does Ginsberg's.

For by the fifties the conversion from pantheism to Christianity which made Everson into Antoninus had given his poetry new energy and a new emphasis. The early struggles for personal identity, intensified by the traumas of the war years, the dissolution of the first marriage, and the complicated relationship with Mary Fabilli, found neither comfort nor resolution in the impersonal God of pantheism and the "inhumanist" philosophy of Jeffers, which required the sacrifice of the personal ego to natural process. The Judaic scriptures saw God as a person, and the Christian tradition as a Trinity of persons whose inter-relationship was enacted in God's dynamic engagement with His created world, most explicitly in Jesus' Incarnation to live mortal life out to death and resurrection. As the central Christian mystery, the Incarnation revealed the union of divinity and humanity from all eternity and, consequently, the redemption of men and women *in* their humanity, body and soul, one by one, as they suffer out through time their integration and transfiguration. The Lawrentian and Jeffersian pantheism of the thirties became caught up in the exploration of Christian erotic mysticism as the radical consequence of, and manifestation of, the Incarnation in our experience of self and other in nature.

Mystics and spiritual writers have, of course, consistently resorted to erotic language and sexual imagery to express the experience of the Beatific Vision, but when theological commentators who have spoken of the sexual act as analogue, even the fullest human analogue, for the experience of God, they have tended thereby to keep the categories of grace and nature safely distinct as terms of an analogy; sex functions as metaphor, a figure of speech for the union with God. But the poetry written by Antoninus in the monastery and by Everson since leaving it

273

participates more deeply in the mystical tradition by pressing the implications of the Incarnation beyond figurative language to perceived and experienced reality. The language of the poetry seeks to be symbolic rather than metaphorical, typological rather than tropological, and the poems—almost always tormented, frequently dizzying, often sublime—stand as the record of stress pitched at and intimating transcendence. Without claiming the insight of the great mystics, Everson/Antoninus sought the imaginative terms, after Whitman and Lawrence and Jeffers, after Freud and Jung, for an erotic mysticism for which the crucifixion enacted, not just once historically but daily in human experience, the agonized cross-point of ecstatic resolution.

With the progression of its three verse paragraphs, "In All These Acts" moves from a graphic account of the death and disembowelment of a buck elk in an avalanche, through a pantheistic assimilation of the mutilated and castrated buck back into the ongoing cycles of natural process, to a vision of Christ in this and every event, "pitched forward/ On the crucifying stroke, juvescent, that will spring Him/Out of the germ, out of the belly of the dying buck,/Out of the father-phallus and the torn-up root." The progression of the verse paragraphs traces out the pattern: the violent erotics of death, the maternal renewal, the transcendent divinity that is the source and motive–power and end of the mortal round.

The language of "The Cross Tore a Hole" is even more shocking because Christ Himself has displaced the buck as the object of contemplation. At one point "the seed sack of Christ's body" on the phallic Tree erupts at death into an orgiastic drench of love into the earth's womb, and so, says the poet, into "my womb":

> My soul,
> God's womb, is seeded
> Of God's own.
>
> My womb,
> God's own, is sown
> Of God's seed.

> My soul,
> Wombed of God's wonder,
> Is seeded, sown.

The three deceptively simple sentences, each beginning with "My" and a noun subject completed by a present tense, passive verb and an "of" phrase, turn the terms of opposition round and round and inside out till the oppositions fall away: the soul enwombed and the womb ensouled; "In Thee, God,/I am Thou," God enfleshed.

In "A Canticle to the Christ in the Holy Eucharist" the poet's reception of Christ incarnate, body and blood, in the eucharistic bread and wine is rendered through the baroque conceit of a doe's impregnation by a buck on the wooded slopes of Tamalpais, the mountain that bulks above the Bay area in the shape of a prone woman. The conceit first presents Christ as "the buck that stamps in the thicket" and enters the poet-communicant as the "fallow doe in the deep madrone." However, since the ravishment is also an impregnation, since the wounding turns into a birthing, Christ assumes a double role: not just the rampant buck whose semen quickens the doe, but also (and simultaneously) the doe whose wound gives birth and bleeds the milk to suckle her offspring. In this way the poet can experience Christ as at once progenitor and progenitrix, and experience himself as at once the vessel of grace and the seed-child of grace. Christ becomes, paradoxically, both his father and his mother, and he becomes, inversely by the same paradox, both Christ's bride and Christ's son.

Two representative stanzas from the middle of the poem elaborate these metamorphoses in which, as in previous poems cited, the animal and human and divine converge:

> In my heart you were might. And thy word was the running of rain
> That rinses October. And the sweetwater spring in the rock. And the
>   brook in the crevice.
> Thy word in my heart was the start of the buck that is sourced in the
>   doe.

Thy word was the milk that will be in her dugs, the stir of new life
in them.
You gazed. I stood barren for days, lay fallow for nights.
Thy look was the movement of life, the milk in the young breasts
of mothers.

My mouth was the babe's. You had stamped like the buck in the
manzanita.
My heart was dry as the dugs of the doe in the fall of the year on
Tamalpais.
I sucked thy wound as the fawn sucks milk from the crowning breast of
its mother.
The flow of thy voice in my shrunken heart was the cling of wild
honey,
The honey that bled from the broken comb in the cleft of Tamalpais.

The language here, as always in Everson's work, is intricately rhetorical, but the rhetoric is integral to the performative action of the poem.
The proliferation of nouns trailing prepositional phrases and modifying
clauses spins out and overlays the shifting associations in a palimpsest
of transparencies. The long, insistently anapestic lines press forward
and stretch out as though to prolong and project the reverberance of
sound past the sensuous particulars of image and thus register metaphor as symbol.

Earlier in this essay I described the complementary aspects of Everson's erotic mysticism as spirals in a double helix or interlocking
gyres: he experiences God in transcendence as "He" and God in immanence as "She." Moreover, his dionysian Catholicism stands in stark
contrast to the work and religious attitudes of T. S. Eliot and Robert
Lowell—both, like him, converts: Eliot an Anglo-Catholic from about
the age of forty, Lowell a Roman Catholic during his twenties. The Calvinist, gnostic temperament of Eliot and Lowell, which sought relief in
Catholicism, continued to keep them embroiled in the contention between nature and grace, body and soul, hidden God and sinful humans.
The Christian poetry of both came to its finest and final expression in

books, *Four Quartets* and *Lord Weary's Castle*, that found the redemptive power of the Incarnation in the apocalypse of World War II. Eliot's deep-seated conviction of human fallibility, which has made a bloody mess of history, allowed him to glimpse the Incarnation only as "the hint half guessed, the gift half understood," and he could only stoically await release from the corruption of flesh into a dimension where at last he could grasp the fire and the rose as one. Lowell strained to sustain his will to believe but could imagine the Incarnation only in terms of the annihilation rather than the redemption of humanity. In "Colloquy in Black Rock," for example, he imagines Christ walking *on* the fouled waters of creation rather than plunging into baptismal immersion, Christ divebombing His warring people and blasting them to bits. Not long after "Colloquy," Lowell left the Church to continue his colloquy with his unappeased soul in elegaic jeremiads of secular damnation.

However, though Everson's Norwegian grandfather had founded the evangelical Iversonians, the conversions of 1934 and 1948 carried him far beyond his Protestant heritage. He emerged from the Second World War and the ruins of his first marriage to sacramentalize the erotic mysticism first imbibed from Jeffers and Lawrence through his Catholic faith, illuminated by scripture and theology, psychology and the accounts of the mystics. His exploration of the convolutions of erotic mysticism has made him, in my judgment, the most important and original Christian poet in English during the second half of the century, as Eliot was for the first. But where Eliot's Christianity was ascetic, conservative, and apollonian—"masculine," if you will—Everson/Antoninus' is radically "feminine," incarnational, and dionysian. It risks itself to the implications of the Incarnation in a way that Eliot could not countenance and Lowell failed to achieve. And for that reason the poetry of Everson/Antoninus is psychologically, emotionally, and theologically bolder and more liberating than theirs, at once more disturbing and more consoling, more violent and more healing.

A fitting epigraph for his work might be the lines that conclude a short poem he wrote as Antoninus about "The South Coast," where Everson now lives at Kingfisher Flat:

> God *makes*. On earth, in us, most instantly,
> On the very now,
> His own means conceives.
> How many strengths break out unchoked
> Where He, Whom all declares,
> Delights to make be!

The Spirit's delight in insemination and gestation, the flesh's declaration of Spirit: the double helix of Everson's erotic mysticism. And the lovely pun on "clarus/light" that turns the last lines at "declares,/Delights" sums up Everson's poetics as it metamorphoses language into vision and gives vision material and verbal form: again, now on the aesthetic level, the double helix of Incarnation.

About the Editor

Albert Gelpi is the Willlliam Robertson Coe Professor of American Literature at Stanford University. His books include *Emily Dickinson: The Mind of the Poet, The Tenth Muse: The Psyche of the American Poet,* and *A Coherent Splendor: The American Poetic Renaissance 1910– 1950.* He's also edited *Wallace Stevens: The Poetics of Modernism, Denise Levertov: Selected Criticism,* and, with Barbara Charlesworth Gelpi, *Adrienne Rich's Poetry and Prose.* He makes his home in Stanford, California.

Design by Ken Sánchez.

Text set in Plantin Light by
Blue Fescue Typography and Design,
Seattle, Washington.